Travel Guide to

Alsace 2024

Historic Castles, Scenic Routes, and Gastronomic Delights

Adam O. Frady

CONTENTS

A Journey through Alsace

Embarking on a journey to Alsace, the northeastern region of France renowned for its half-timbered houses, picturesque villages, and exceptional wines, felt like stepping into a storybook. Nestled between the Rhine River and the Vosges Mountains, Alsace is a blend of French and Germanic influences, offering a unique cultural tapestry that beckoned me to explore its winding streets and savor its culinary delights.

Arrival in Strasbourg

I arrived in Strasbourg, the capital of Alsace, on a crisp autumn morning. The city welcomed me with its blend of Gothic architecture and modern vibrancy. My first stop was the Strasbourg Cathedral, an awe-inspiring Gothic masterpiece that towered over the cityscape. The intricate façade, adorned with sculptures and gargoyles, captivated me for hours. Climbing the spiral staircase to the cathedral's platform, I was rewarded with panoramic views of Strasbourg, the Rhine River, and the Black Forest beyond.

Strolling through the Petite France district, I found myself enchanted by the half-timbered houses lining the canals. The reflection of these charming buildings in the water, combined with the autumn foliage, created a scene of such picturesque beauty that it felt almost surreal. I lingered in this quarter, savoring a leisurely lunch at a traditional winstub, a local wine tavern. The choucroute garnie, a dish of sauerkraut and various meats, paired with a crisp Riesling, introduced me to the region's culinary traditions.

Exploring the Wine Route

Leaving Strasbourg behind, I embarked on the Route des Vins d'Alsace, the famed Alsace Wine Route. This scenic journey took me through rolling vineyards, medieval villages, and historic castles, each stop revealing a new facet of Alsace's rich heritage. My first destination was Obernai, a quaint town with cobblestone streets and colorful houses. The town's central square, Place du Marché, was bustling with a market where local vendors sold cheeses, pastries, and, of course, wines. I sampled a glass of Gewürztraminer, a fragrant, slightly sweet wine that tingled my taste buds and evoked the essence of Alsace.

Continuing my journey, I reached Ribeauvillé, a village nestled at the foot of the Vosges Mountains. Known for its three medieval castles, Ribeauvillé exuded an old-world charm. I spent the afternoon hiking up to the ruins of Château de Saint-Ulrich, where the sweeping views of the vineyards below were nothing short of breathtaking. Back in the village, I visited a local winery, where a friendly vintner guided me through a tasting of Pinot Blanc and Pinot Gris, explaining the distinct terroir that makes Alsace wines so special.

The Enchantment of Colmar

My next stop was Colmar, often hailed as the "Capital of Alsatian Wine." Stepping into Colmar felt like stepping into a fairy tale. The old town's narrow streets were lined with half-timbered houses painted in a palette of pastel colors. The Little Venice district, with its charming canals and flower-adorned bridges, was particularly enchanting. I wandered through the streets, marveling at the whimsical architecture and the vibrant atmosphere of the weekly market.

In Colmar, I visited the Unterlinden Museum, housed in a former convent. The museum's collection of medieval and Renaissance art, including the famous Isenheim Altarpiece, provided a deep dive into the region's artistic heritage. Afterward, I indulged in a tarte flambée, a thin-crust Alsatian pizza topped with cream, onions, and lardons, accompanied by a glass of dry Muscat wine.

The combination of flavors, both simple and exquisite, reflected the essence of Alsatian cuisine.

The Castles of Alsace

Eager to delve into the region's history, I set out to explore some of Alsace's storied castles. Haut-Koenigsbourg Castle, perched high on a hill, offered a glimpse into medieval life. The castle, meticulously restored in the early 20th century, provided a fascinating tour through its grand halls, armories, and battlements. The panoramic views from the castle's towers, overlooking the Alsace plain and the Black Forest, were awe-inspiring.

Another highlight was Château du Haut-Barr, known as the "Eye of Alsace" for its strategic vantage point. Accessible via a narrow footbridge, the castle ruins provided a thrilling sense of adventure. I spent hours exploring the ancient walls and imagining the lives of those who once inhabited this lofty fortress.

The Essence of Alsatian Cuisine

No trip to Alsace would be complete without indulging in its culinary delights. In addition to the traditional dishes I had already sampled, I was keen to explore more of the region's gastronomic offerings. In the village of Eguisheim, I discovered a charming restaurant that specialized in Baeckeoffe, a hearty casserole of marinated meats and potatoes slow-cooked in a clay pot. The rich, savory flavors, enhanced by the local wine used in the marinade, made for a satisfying meal that warmed me from the inside out.

I also had the opportunity to participate in a cooking class in Kaysersberg, where I learned to prepare kugelhopf, a traditional Alsatian cake. The process of kneading the dough, incorporating raisins and almonds, and baking it in a distinctive Bundt pan was both educational and enjoyable. The result, a golden, aromatic cake with a slightly sweet flavor, was a perfect treat to accompany my afternoon coffee.

Nature's Splendor

While Alsace is renowned for its vineyards and villages, its natural landscapes are equally captivating. I ventured into the Vosges Mountains, where a network of hiking trails offered a chance to explore the region's rugged beauty. The trails led me through dense forests, past tranquil lakes, and up to high peaks with panoramic views. One of the highlights was a hike to Lac Blanc, a pristine alpine lake surrounded by rocky cliffs and pine trees. The serene beauty of the lake, reflecting the blue sky and the autumn foliage, provided a perfect backdrop for a picnic lunch.

In contrast, a visit to the Ballons des Vosges Nature Park revealed the diverse ecosystems of the region. Here, I encountered wildflower meadows, ancient forests, and rolling hills dotted with grazing cows. The park's visitor center provided insights into the local flora and fauna, enriching my understanding of the natural heritage of Alsace.

Reflecting on Alsace

As my journey through Alsace drew to a close, I found myself reflecting on the rich tapestry of experiences I had woven. From the bustling streets of Strasbourg to the tranquil vineyards of the Wine Route, from the medieval castles to the modern art of Colmar, Alsace had revealed itself as a region of contrasts and harmonies. The blend of French and Germanic influences, the interplay of tradition and modernity, and the seamless integration of natural beauty and cultural heritage had created a journey that was both enriching and unforgettable.

Each village, each vineyard, each dish, and each view had contributed to a symphony of sights, sounds, and flavors that lingered in my memory. As I boarded the train to return home, I carried with me not just souvenirs and photographs, but a deep appreciation for the region's unique character and a longing to one day return to the enchanting land of Alsace.

Introduction

History and Geography

Alsace boasts a captivating narrative woven from centuries of historical events and diverse geographical features. Its strategic location at the crossroads of major European powers has rendered it a coveted territory, resulting in a unique cultural fusion that sets it apart.

The story of Alsace begins in ancient times, with evidence of Neanderthal presence dating back hundreds of thousands of years. As time progressed, various groups of early humans left their mark on the region, culminating in the establishment of farming communities during the Neolithic period. The fertile soils of Alsace, nourished by the Ill River and sheltered by the Vosges Mountains, proved ideal for cultivating crops and raising livestock.

However, the region's true identity as an early medieval pagus emerged after the fall of the Roman Empire. Alsace became a coveted prize for numerous kingdoms and empires, including the Alamanni, Franks, Lotharingians, and the Holy Roman Empire. The constant power struggles between France and Germany over

Alsace left an indelible mark on its history, as exemplified by the Franco-Prussian War and the two World Wars. This tug-of-war for control significantly shaped the region's cultural landscape and political affiliations.

Geographically, Alsace's position is defined by the imposing Vosges Mountains to the west and the meandering Rhine River to the east. This distinctive topography has contributed to Alsace's reputation as one of central Europe's most fertile regions. The Vosges Mountains, cloaked in dense forests of fir, beech, and oak, provide a scenic backdrop to the region's agricultural abundance. The relatively low annual precipitation ensures favorable conditions for farming and viticulture.

The plain of Alsace, stretching eastward from the Vosges, is renowned for its intensive agriculture. The foothills of the mountains are carpeted with vineyards, producing exceptional white wines such as Riesling and Gewürztraminer, which have garnered international acclaim. The alluvial plain, particularly west of Strasbourg, is devoted to the cultivation of cereals, sugar beets, hops, and tobacco. Alsace is also celebrated for its delectable asparagus and foie gras, sought-after delicacies that reflect the region's rich culinary heritage.

Beyond agriculture, Alsace boasts a robust and diversified industrial economy. The city of Mulhouse has a long-standing tradition of textile manufacturing, while the region's modern industries encompass automobile assembly, pharmaceuticals, electronics, and telecommunications. This economic diversity has fostered a vibrant and resilient community.

Alsace's cultural identity is a fascinating blend of French and German influences. Its architecture showcases a harmonious fusion of styles, while the local dialect, Alsatian, is a testament to the region's linguistic diversity. Strasbourg, the capital of Alsace, stands as a symbol of European unity, playing host to several important European institutions.

The culinary traditions of Alsace are equally captivating, reflecting the region's dual heritage. Choucroute garnie, a hearty dish of sauerkraut and various meats, and tarte flambée, a thin-crust pizza-like creation, are prime examples of the culinary fusion found in Alsace. These dishes, and many others, highlight the unique flavors and techniques that have emerged from the region's complex history and cultural exchange.

Alsace's captivating story is one of resilience, adaptability, and cultural richness. Its strategic location, diverse geography, and tumultuous history have all contributed to the formation of a truly unique identity. From ancient human settlements to modern industrial prowess, from the fertile plains to the majestic mountains, Alsace continues to enchant and inspire those who have the privilege of experiencing its wonders.

Top Reasons to Visit

The harmonious blend of French and German influences, coupled with breathtaking landscapes and a rich culture, make it a destination that promises an unforgettable experience.

One of the most iconic landmarks in Alsace is the majestic Strasbourg Cathedral, a true masterpiece of Gothic architecture. Its towering presence once dominated the skyline as the tallest building in the world, and its intricate stonework and resplendent stained-glass windows continue to awe visitors today. The astronomical clock within the cathedral is a marvel of medieval engineering, while ascending the tower unveils panoramic views of the city below, leaving a lasting impression on all who venture to its heights.

Another gem that awaits discovery in Alsace is the enchanting town of Colmar. Often referred to as a fairytale town, Colmar's medieval center boasts cobblestone streets lined with charming half-timbered houses adorned with colorful flowers. The district of Petite Venice, with its picturesque canals and vibrantly decorated houses, further enhances the town's magical ambiance. Visitors can embark on a delightful paddle boat ride or leisurely cruise along the La Lauch river, immersing themselves in the romantic atmosphere.

Within Strasbourg itself, the Petite France district is a UNESCO World Heritage site that exudes charm and history. The half-timbered houses, leaning precariously over the canals, once served as homes for fishermen and millers, their livelihoods dependent on the waterways that crisscrossed the area. Today, Petite France is a haven for those seeking a taste of traditional Alsatian cuisine, with its quaint restaurants and cafes offering delectable regional specialties.

For wine enthusiasts, the Alsace Wine Route is an absolute must. This scenic journey winds through vineyards that produce some of the world's most renowned white wines, including Riesling and Gewürztraminer. Along the way, visitors can stop at charming towns and villages, each with its unique character and wineries offering tastings and insights into the art of winemaking. It's a sensory adventure that delights the palate and enriches the soul.

Beyond the bustling cities and towns, Alsace is dotted with picturesque villages that seem to have sprung from the pages of a storybook. Eguisheim and Riquewihr are just two examples of these idyllic havens, where time seems to slow down. Their vibrant flower displays, historic architecture, and warm hospitality create an inviting atmosphere that encourages exploration and relaxation.

Food lovers will find themselves in paradise in Alsace, where the culinary traditions are a delightful fusion of German and French influences. Hearty dishes like choucroute garnie, a savory sauerkraut stew, and baeckeoffe, a slow-cooked meat and vegetable casserole, showcase the region's agricultural abundance and culinary creativity. Tarte flambée, a thin-crust pizza-like creation, is another regional specialty that tantalizes the taste buds.

During the holiday season, Alsace transforms into a magical wonderland, with some of the most enchanting Christmas markets in Europe. The festive atmosphere, with its twinkling lights, festive decorations, and enticing aromas, creates a sense of wonder and joy. The markets offer a treasure trove of handcrafted gifts, seasonal treats, and mulled wine, making them a perfect place to soak up the holiday spirit.

Nature enthusiasts will be equally captivated by Alsace's diverse landscapes. The Vosges Mountains, with their rolling hills and verdant forests, offer ample opportunities for hiking, biking, and other outdoor activities. The fertile plains, with their patchwork of fields and vineyards, provide a serene and picturesque setting for leisurely strolls or picnics.

The unique blend of French and German cultures in Alsace is evident in every aspect of life, from the architecture to the language and traditions. This cultural fusion has created a distinct identity that is both intriguing and welcoming. Visitors are often charmed by the warmth and hospitality of the locals, who are proud to share their heritage with the world.

With its easy accessibility from major European cities and a well-developed infrastructure, Alsace is a convenient and enjoyable destination for travelers. Whether you're interested in history, culture, cuisine, or outdoor adventures, Alsace has something to offer everyone. Its unique blend of attractions, coupled with the warm hospitality of its people, ensures that a visit to Alsace will be an experience to cherish.

Getting to Alsace

By Plane

With its strategic location, Alsace benefits from excellent air connectivity through two major international airports, offering convenient options for both domestic and international visitors.

The primary gateway to Alsace is Strasbourg Airport (SXB), conveniently located southwest of Strasbourg city. This bustling airport serves as a hub for numerous flights connecting major French cities like Paris, Marseille, Nice, and Toulouse. Travelers can reach Strasbourg from these cities in approximately an hour, making it a swift and efficient journey. Moreover, Strasbourg Airport also provides connections to other European destinations, ensuring that travelers from various parts of the continent can easily reach Alsace.

Another significant airport serving the region is the Basel-Mulhouse EuroAirport (BSL/MLH/EAP), situated near the borders of Switzerland and Germany. This unique tri-national airport caters to the travel needs of Basel in Switzerland, Mulhouse in France, and Freiburg in Germany. With a wide range of flight options, travelers can access major European cities like

Amsterdam, Berlin, London, Rome, Barcelona, and Madrid from this airport. Flight durations to these destinations typically range from one hour and fifteen minutes to one hour and fifty minutes, providing flexibility and convenience for travelers with varying schedules.

Upon arrival at Strasbourg Airport, travelers can quickly reach the city center by train in just ten minutes, making the transfer smooth and hassle-free. Similarly, from Basel-Mulhouse EuroAirport, a dedicated shuttle service operates regular connections to the Saint-Louis train station, from where travelers can continue their journey into Alsace's captivating towns and villages.

Both Strasbourg and Basel-Mulhouse airports offer a comprehensive range of facilities to enhance the travel experience. Travelers can avail themselves of car rental services for convenient exploration of the region at their own pace. Currency exchange services are readily available for those needing to convert their money, while duty-free shops offer a chance to indulge in some retail therapy before or after their flight.

Planning a trip to Alsace by air is a breeze, with numerous national and international airlines operating flights to the region. Travelers can utilize online travel agents and flight comparison websites to research and book the most suitable flights based on their budget and itinerary. These platforms often provide detailed information on flight schedules, prices, and available airlines, empowering travelers to make informed decisions.

Before embarking on your journey to Alsace, it's crucial to consider a few essential aspects. Firstly, depending on your nationality, you may need a visa to enter France. It's essential to check the visa requirements well in advance and ensure you have the necessary documentation. Additionally, purchasing travel insurance that covers flight cancellations, delays, and medical emergencies is highly recommended for a worry-free trip.

Since Alsace experiences a continental climate with warm summers and cold winters, packing appropriate clothing for the season is crucial. It's also advisable to familiarize yourself with the airport facilities, such as restaurants, lounges, and other amenities, to ensure a comfortable and enjoyable travel experience.

By Train

Traveling to Alsace by train is not merely a means of transportation; it's an immersive experience that unveils the region's captivating history and scenic landscapes. The train routes leading to this enchanting destination offer a glimpse into the heart of Europe, making the journey as rewarding as the destination itself.

Alsace's principal rail hubs are Strasbourg, its vibrant capital, and Mulhouse, another significant city in the region. These well-connected cities serve as gateways to Alsace, with numerous high-speed and regional train services linking them to major European cities. This extensive network ensures that travelers from near and far can easily reach Alsace by train, embarking on a memorable adventure.

One of the most popular routes is the high-speed TGV (Train à Grande Vitesse) connection between Paris and Strasbourg. This remarkable train service whisks passengers from the bustling French capital to the charming Alsatian heartland in a mere one hour and forty-six minutes. With frequent departures throughout the day, the TGV caters to both leisure travelers and business professionals, providing a fast and convenient option for reaching Alsace.

Alsace's strategic location also makes it easily accessible from other European countries. Direct high-speed trains from Brussels to Strasbourg, for instance, complete the journey in approximately three hours and thirty minutes, while connections from Luxembourg take even less time, clocking in at around one hour and thirty-five minutes. Travelers from Germany can also reach Alsace with ease, as Frankfurt is just one hour and forty-eight minutes away by train, and even Munich is accessible in approximately three hours and thirty minutes.

The train journey to Alsace is not solely about speed and efficiency; it's an opportunity to soak in the region's picturesque landscapes. As the train traverses the French countryside, passengers are treated to a visual feast. The scenery gradually transforms from the flat expanses of the Paris Basin to the undulating hills and sun-drenched vineyards of Champagne and Lorraine. Finally, the imposing Vosges Mountains emerge on the horizon, signaling the imminent arrival in the enchanting region of Alsace.

Upon reaching Strasbourg or Mulhouse, travelers can seamlessly transfer to local TER (Transport Express Régional) trains, which offer extensive coverage throughout the region. These convenient connections allow for easy exploration of Alsace's numerous towns and villages. For instance, the journey from Strasbourg to Colmar, renowned for its captivating architecture and winemaking heritage, takes a mere thirty minutes. Similarly, reaching Mulhouse from Colmar is a quick and effortless twenty-minute train ride.

When planning your train journey to Alsace, it's highly recommended to book tickets in advance, especially during peak travel seasons such as summer and the festive Christmas markets. The SNCF website, along with various other train ticket platforms, provide user-friendly booking options. By booking early, travelers can often secure the best deals and ensure a smooth and stress-free journey.

Before boarding the train, it's essential to consider a few practical tips. Checking the train schedules is crucial, as they can vary depending on the day and time of travel. Packing light is also advisable, as it makes navigating train stations and storing luggage on board more convenient. Additionally, arriving at the station early allows ample time for checking in, finding your platform, and settling in before the train departs.

By Car

Embarking on a road trip to Alsace promises an unforgettable adventure, granting travelers the autonomy to uncover the region's allure at their own leisurely pace. Whether you're setting off from a neighboring European country or venturing from a distant corner of the globe, the journey to Alsace by car is an experience brimming with anticipation and scenic splendor.

Alsace's strategic location within the European road network ensures easy accessibility for those arriving by car. Sharing borders with Germany and Switzerland, the region is traversed by two prominent motorways—the A35, which extends north-south alongside the Rhine valley, and the A4, connecting to Paris and other regions of eastern France.

For travelers originating from neighboring countries, the pathways to Alsace are well-defined.

- **Germany:** The A5 autobahn in Germany seamlessly transitions into the A35 motorway in France, making the drive from Frankfurt to Alsace a mere 2 hours and 15 minutes.

- **Switzerland:** Swiss travelers can utilize the A3 motorway, which connects to the French A35, enabling a journey from Zurich or Bern to Alsace in approximately 1 hour and 30 minutes.
- **Belgium:** Those departing from Brussels can opt for the A4 motorway, anticipating a travel time of roughly 4 hours and 30 minutes to reach their Alsatian destination.
- **Italy:** The drive from Milan to Alsace involves utilizing the A5 in Italy and transitioning to the A35 in France, with an estimated travel time of 4 hours and 30 minutes.
- **Austria:** Vienna, situated further afield, requires a longer journey of approximately 8 hours and 30 minutes, typically involving the A4 and A35 motorways.

The allure of a road trip to Alsace lies in the ability to savor scenic routes and make spontaneous stops. The Vosges Mountains, particularly enchanting during autumn when the forests are ablaze with color, offer picturesque drives. The Alsace Wine Route, a winding path through charming wine villages and past historic castles, is an essential addition to any itinerary.

Thorough preparation is key to a smooth and enjoyable road trip.
- **Vehicle Readiness:** Prioritize a comprehensive check of your vehicle, ensuring tires, brakes, and fluids are in optimal condition.

- **Navigation:** Equip yourself with a dependable GPS system or up-to-date maps to navigate the European roads confidently.
- **Legal Requirements:** Familiarize yourself with the driving regulations in France and any countries you'll traverse, encompassing tolls, speed limits, and mandatory equipment such as reflective vests and warning triangles.
- **Rest Stops:** Plan for regular breaks to combat fatigue, especially during extended stretches of the journey.

Upon reaching Alsace, you'll discover a driver-friendly region characterized by well-maintained roads and clear signage. Parking is generally readily available in cities and towns, though it may be more limited in popular tourist destinations during peak seasons.

Local Transportation Options

Alsace offers a diverse and efficient network of local transportation options to facilitate both residents and visitors in exploring its multifaceted landscapes. From historic cities to picturesque villages, and from vineyards to mountain peaks, Alsace's transportation network ensures a seamless and enjoyable travel experience.

Regional Trains (TER): The backbone of Alsace's public transportation is its extensive regional train network, referred to as TER (Transport Express Régional). This network encompasses 14 railway lines and 161 stations, effectively linking major urban centers like Strasbourg and Mulhouse with smaller towns and rural communities scattered throughout the region. A notable feature of the TER network is its synchronization with coach schedules, enabling convenient transfers and providing comprehensive coverage across Alsace. Moreover, the TER network caters to cyclists by allowing them to take their bikes on trains for free, with the exception of rush hour periods between Strasbourg and Basel.

High-Speed Trains (TGV): For those seeking swift travel between major cities, the high-speed train (TGV) serves as an excellent choice. It operates between Basel, Mulhouse, and Strasbourg, significantly reducing travel time and enhancing connectivity within Alsace. The TGV is particularly appealing to travelers who wish to maximize their time in the region or embark on day trips to neighboring areas.

Tramways in Strasbourg: Strasbourg boasts a modern and efficient tramway system comprising six lines (A through F).

This network effectively connects the city center with its outskirts, providing convenient access to popular attractions and neighborhoods.

Notable destinations served by the tramway include the iconic Notre-Dame Cathedral, the vibrant Place Kléber, the charming Petite France District, the historic Palais Rohan, and the significant European Quarter. The tramway's operational hours extend from early morning until after midnight, affording visitors ample time to explore the city's diverse offerings.

Buses and Inter-City Coaches: Alsace's transportation network is further augmented by a comprehensive system of buses and inter-city coaches. These modes of transportation effectively complement the train services by connecting areas not directly accessible by rail.

Additionally, bus schedules are often coordinated with train arrivals and departures, facilitating smooth transfers for travelers. For those venturing beyond the major cities, buses offer a valuable means of reaching the region's numerous picturesque villages and natural attractions.

Cycling and Walking: Alsace's commitment to sustainable transportation is evident in its extensive network of dedicated paths and routes designed for cyclists and pedestrians. Exploring the region by bicycle or on foot allows for a more immersive and leisurely experience, enabling travelers to savor the picturesque scenery and cultural nuances at their own pace. Whether cycling through vineyards or strolling along the canals of Strasbourg, these modes of transportation offer a unique perspective on Alsace's allure.

Peak Route Shuttle: During the summer months, the Peak Route shuttle provides a specialized service that transports nature enthusiasts and hikers to the summits of the Vosges Mountains. This service is particularly attractive to those who wish to experience the region's spectacular natural landscapes without the need for a private vehicle.

Car Rentals: For travelers who prioritize the flexibility and independence afforded by driving, Alsace offers an efficient motorway system and readily available car rental services. The A35 motorway traverses Alsace from north to south, ensuring convenient access to various parts of the region. Furthermore, smaller roads provide scenic routes through picturesque villages and along the renowned Alsace Wine Route.

Tips for Utilizing Local Transportation: To ensure a smooth and efficient travel experience in Alsace, consider the following tips:

- Plan your itinerary in advance, taking advantage of online tools like Fluo Grand Est to identify the most suitable combination of public transportation options for your specific needs.
- Purchase tickets in advance or utilize contactless payment options to expedite your boarding process and avoid unnecessary delays.
- Rest assured that most public transportation options in Alsace are designed to accommodate visitors with disabilities, guaranteeing a comfortable and inclusive travel experience for all.

Use this website to have a perfect budget for your trip to Alsace France: **https://www.budgetyourtrip.com**

Best Time to Visit

Seasonal Highlights

Every season in Alsace unveils a new facet of its allure, beckoning visitors with unique festivals, landscapes, and traditions.

Spring in Alsace: As the grip of winter loosens, Alsace awakens to the vibrant hues of spring. From mid to late spring, the region's vineyards gradually shed their winter dormancy, revealing the first delicate green shoots that promise a bountiful harvest. Wildflowers begin to pepper the countryside, transforming the landscape into a breathtaking tapestry of colors. The mild temperatures of spring make it an ideal time to partake in outdoor activities such as hiking and cycling, particularly along the renowned Alsace Wine Route, which comes to life after its winter respite.

Summer Delights: The arrival of summer ushers in a period of warmth, merriment, and cultural celebrations in Alsace. Throughout June, July, and August, the region's towns and villages host a myriad of lively festivals, many of which revolve around the bountiful summer harvest. The Alsace Wine Route becomes a hub of cultural exploration, with wineries extending invitations to exclusive tastings and the streets resonating with the melodies of live music, the rhythmic movements of folk dancers, and a diverse array of events that showcase the region's unique heritage.

Autumn: Autumn casts a magical spell over Alsace, transforming its landscapes into a breathtaking canvas of golds, reds, and browns. The vineyards take on a golden hue as the grapes ripen, and the forests of the Vosges Mountains become ablaze with fiery foliage. The autumn harvest brings a sense of abundance to the region, with markets overflowing with fresh produce, including the prized grapes that contribute to Alsace's world-renowned wines. The region's majestic castles, perched atop verdant hills and often veiled in a mystical shroud of mist, become even more enchanting against the backdrop of the autumn sky.

Winter Wonderland: Alsace's reputation for hosting some of Europe's most exquisite Christmas markets is well-deserved. From late November through December, towns like Strasbourg and Colmar undergo a remarkable transformation into veritable winter wonderlands. Twinkling lights adorn every corner, festive decorations create an atmosphere of warmth and cheer, and charming stalls overflow with handcrafted treasures and seasonal delicacies. The air is perfumed with the enticing aromas of mulled wine and gingerbread, making it an undeniably magical time to experience the region's unique charm.

Year-Round Attractions: Alsace's allure extends beyond its seasonal festivities, offering a plethora of attractions that captivate visitors throughout the year. The Strasbourg Cathedral, a masterpiece of Gothic architecture, stands as a testament to the region's rich history and artistic achievements. Its intricate stonework, soaring spires, and remarkable astronomical clock leave a lasting impression on all who visit. The medieval center of Colmar, with its enchanting half-timbered houses, picturesque canals, and vibrant flower boxes, exudes timeless charm regardless of the season. The Petite France district in Strasbourg, a UNESCO World Heritage site, transports visitors back in time with its quaint streets, charming bridges, and well-preserved architecture that reflects the region's soul.

Festivals and Events

Spring Festivals: As the first signs of spring emerge, Alsace awakens with a series of festive events that embrace the season of renewal. Easter markets, scattered throughout various towns, showcase traditional decorations, local crafts, and an array of seasonal treats, including chocolate eggs and the beloved Osterlammele, a lamb-shaped cake traditionally enjoyed during Easter. The Fête du Printemps, or Spring Festival, held in towns like Colmar, marks the end of winter's embrace with a burst of color and merriment. Flower markets fill the streets with fragrant blooms, while folk dances and the tantalizing aromas of regional specialties add to the festive ambiance.

Summer Celebrations: The summer months in Alsace are a time of joyous celebrations, often centered around the region's renowned wine culture. The Fête de la Musique, a nationwide celebration of music held on June 21st, fills the streets of Alsatian cities with melodies of all genres as musicians take to the stage. Wine festivals, a highlight of the summer season, take place in various wine-producing villages, each boasting its own unique charm. These festivals offer wine enthusiasts the opportunity to indulge in tastings, witness lively parades, and witness the crowning of the local wine queen, a symbol of the region's winemaking heritage.

Autumn Events: As summer fades into autumn, Alsace prepares for the bountiful harvest season. The Colmar Wine Fair, held in August, stands as a prominent event in the region's wine calendar. This grand fair showcases a diverse selection of Alsatian wines and champagnes, attracting connoisseurs and enthusiasts from near and far. In October, the Festival of New Wine, also known as the "Fête du Vin Nouveau," celebrates the year's harvest with freshly fermented wines, accompanied by traditional tarts and lively music.

Winter Wonders: Winter in Alsace is synonymous with enchantment, and the region's Christmas markets are a testament to this magical season. Strasbourg, in particular, hosts one of Europe's oldest and largest Christmas markets, transforming the city into a dazzling wonderland of lights, decorations, and festive cheer. Saint Nicholas Day, celebrated on December 6th, honors the region's patron saint with processions, sweet treats, and gifts for children.

Cultural Events: Alsace's cultural calendar is punctuated by events that cater to a diverse range of interests. The Strasbourg Film Festival, a platform for European and international cinema, attracts filmmakers and film enthusiasts alike. Jazz lovers can revel in the Colmar Jazz Festival, which showcases the talents of renowned artists and emerging stars in the intimate setting of Colmar's historic venues.

Traditional Alsatian Festivals: Alsace's unique cultural heritage is reflected in its traditional festivals, which offer a glimpse into the region's history and customs. The Fête des Ménétriers, or Fiddlers' Festival, held in Ribeauvillé, is a medieval-themed event that features musicians, dancers, and jesters adorned in traditional costumes. This festival pays homage to the town's historical privileges granted to minstrels. Pfifferdaj, celebrated in Ribeauvillé, is the oldest festival in Alsace, transporting the town back to the Middle Ages with a grand parade, a bustling medieval market, and thrilling jousting tournaments.

Unique to Alsace: Alsace also boasts unique festivals that celebrate the region's natural wonders and artisanal traditions. The Stork Festival, held to commemorate the return of the storks, symbolizes spring and rebirth, featuring stork-themed events and educational activities. Pottery markets, held in villages like Soufflenheim and Betschdorf, showcase the region's rich ceramic heritage, offering visitors a chance to admire and acquire beautifully crafted pottery and ceramic wares.

https://www.visit.alsace/en/

Explore Alsace Official Tourism Website to View beautiful Alsace Landscape/tourist destinations and other services you will need in Alsace.

Exploring the Regions

Northern Alsace

Northern Alsace, an alluring region nestled in the northeastern corner of France, stands as a hidden gem for those seeking an authentic and enriching travel experience. Often overlooked in favor of its more renowned southern counterpart, Northern Alsace boasts a harmonious blend of historical significance, natural splendor, and cultural vibrancy. Let us embark on a journey to uncover the treasures that this captivating region has to offer.

Geographical Setting: The geographical tapestry of Northern Alsace is a testament to nature's artistry. The region's landscape is characterized by a delightful contrast between the verdant forests of the Vosges Mountains and the tranquil embrace of the Rhine River. This juxtaposition of rugged terrain and serene waters creates a captivating backdrop for exploration and adventure. Northern Alsace's location, bordering Germany to the east and the Lorraine region to the west, has fostered a unique cultural fusion that is evident in its architecture, traditions, and cuisine.

Historical Significance: The historical narrative of Northern Alsace is both rich and complex. Throughout the centuries, this region has witnessed a tumultuous past, with control shifting between French and German hands. This historical tug-of-war has left an indelible mark on the region's cultural identity and architectural landscape. The remnants of its strategic past are evident in the numerous castles and fortifications that punctuate the landscape, each bearing witness to the region's medieval heritage.

Cultural Heritage: Northern Alsace is a haven for traditional craftsmanship, where time-honored skills have been passed down through generations. The region's artisans are celebrated for their expertise in pottery-making, a craft that has deep roots in the local culture. Visitors have the opportunity to immerse themselves in the world of pottery by exploring charming villages dedicated to this art form and witnessing the creation of exquisite ceramic pieces.

Natural Wonders: The natural environment of Northern Alsace is nothing short of awe-inspiring. The Vosges Mountains, with their dense forests, cascading waterfalls, and breathtaking vistas, offer a paradise for hikers, nature enthusiasts, and outdoor adventurers. The Northern Vosges Regional Nature Park, recognized as a UNESCO Biosphere Reserve, safeguards a remarkable diversity of ecosystems and species, further enhancing the region's natural allure.

Fortified Castles: A hallmark of Northern Alsace is its collection of fortified castles, perched majestically atop pink sandstone bluffs. These architectural marvels, including Fleckenstein Castle and Schoenenbourg Fort, evoke a sense of wonder and offer a glimpse into the region's tumultuous past. As sentinels overlooking the landscape, these castles serve as a poignant reminder of the region's medieval heritage and invite exploration and discovery.

The Maginot Line: The Maginot Line, a series of fortifications constructed along the French-German border in the aftermath of World War I, has left an enduring legacy in Northern Alsace. Today, visitors can traverse the vestiges of this defensive line, ranging from unassuming blockhouses to imposing forts, and gain insights into the region's military history.

Cuisine and Gastronomy: The culinary landscape of Northern Alsace is a reflection of its cultural fusion, harmoniously blending French and German culinary traditions. Local specialties, such as tarte flambée (a thin-crust pizza-like dish), choucroute garnie (sauerkraut with various meats), and baeckeoffe (a hearty meat and potato stew), tantalize the taste buds with their robust flavors and hearty ingredients. The region's brewing heritage is equally noteworthy, with a tradition of beer production that dates back centuries.

Festivals and Events: Throughout the year, Northern Alsace comes alive with a vibrant array of festivals and events that showcase the region's rich cultural tapestry. From the enchanting Christmas markets that illuminate the winter months to the lively summer wine festivals that celebrate the region's viticultural bounty, there is always something happening to captivate and entertain visitors.

Why Visit Northern Alsace? Northern Alsace beckons travelers with its authenticity, warmth, and tranquility. It offers a respite from the fast-paced modern world, inviting visitors to slow down, reconnect with nature, and immerse themselves in the rich tapestry of history and culture. Whether you seek to explore ancient castles, wander through picturesque villages, embark on outdoor adventures, or simply savor the simple pleasures of life,

Northern Alsace promises an unforgettable experience that will leave you with cherished memories.

Central Alsace

Central Alsace beckons travelers with its captivating blend of history, culture, and natural beauty. This enchanting area, with its picturesque villages, rolling vineyards, and architectural gems, encapsulates the essence of French countryside charm. Central Alsace's allure lies in its ability to seamlessly weave together the threads of its past, preserving traditions while embracing the vibrancy of modern life.

History: Central Alsace boasts a rich history, bearing witness to centuries of cultural exchange and political shifts. The region's roots trace back to Roman and early Germanic settlements, leaving behind a legacy that is still visible in its architecture and customs. Over the centuries, Central Alsace was an integral part of the Holy Roman Empire and later found itself at the center of Franco-German conflicts, a history that has contributed to its unique cultural identity.

Geographic Splendor: Nestled between the majestic Vosges Mountains to the west and the meandering Rhine River to the east, Central Alsace enjoys a privileged geographical location. This unique topography creates a microclimate that nurtures the region's renowned vineyards, producing wines that are celebrated worldwide. The rolling hills, dotted with charming villages and verdant vineyards, create a landscape that is as picturesque as it is diverse.

Cultural Mosaic: Central Alsace is a treasure trove of cultural heritage, where traditions are cherished and celebrated. The region's half-timbered houses, with their intricate woodwork and colorful facades, are a testament to its architectural legacy. Medieval castles, perched atop hilltops, offer a glimpse into a bygone era of knights and chivalry. The Alsatian culture, a harmonious blend of French and German influences, is reflected in the local dialect, the hearty cuisine, and the vibrant festivals that punctuate the calendar.

Strasbourg: Strasbourg, the capital of Alsace, is a city that seamlessly blends its historical heritage with modern vibrancy. The city's crown jewel, the Strasbourg Cathedral, is a marvel of Gothic architecture, captivating visitors with its intricate details, including the famous astronomical clock. As the seat of the European Parliament, Strasbourg also plays a crucial role in

European politics, adding a layer of contemporary significance to its historical identity.

Colmar: Colmar, often hailed as the quintessential Alsatian town, is a picture-perfect destination that exudes charm and character. Its well-preserved old town, with its winding canals, flower-laden bridges, and colorful half-timbered houses, feels like a scene from a fairy tale. The Unterlinden Museum, housing a collection of art spanning from the Middle Ages to the 20th century, is a cultural highlight. Colmar's location on the Alsace Wine Route and its renowned Colmar Wine Fair further cement its reputation as a must-visit destination.

The Alsace Wine Route: The Alsace Wine Route is a scenic journey that winds through the heart of Central Alsace, connecting charming wine-producing villages like Riquewihr, Kaysersberg, and Eguisheim. This route offers visitors the opportunity to savor the region's world-class wines through tastings and vineyard tours. The rolling hills, dotted with picturesque villages and vineyards bathed in sunlight, create a landscape that is both breathtaking and inspiring.

Culinary Delights: Central Alsace is a haven for food lovers, with a culinary scene that reflects its rich cultural heritage. Tarte flambée, a thin-crust pizza-like dish topped with crème fraîche, onions, and bacon, is a regional specialty that tantalizes the taste buds. Choucroute garnie, a hearty dish of sauerkraut with various meats, is a staple of Alsatian cuisine. And no visit to the region would be complete without sampling the creamy, pungent Munster cheese.

Festivals and Events: Central Alsace comes alive with a vibrant array of festivals and events throughout the year. The Colmar Wine Fair, a major celebration of the region's winemaking heritage, attracts visitors from around the world. The Strasbourg Christmas Market, one of Europe's oldest and largest, transforms the city into a magical wonderland of lights, decorations, and festive cheer. These are just two examples of the many events that showcase the region's cultural vibrancy and joie de vivre.

Natural Attractions and Artistic Treasures: Beyond its charming towns and villages, Central Alsace boasts a wealth of natural attractions and artistic treasures. The Vosges Mountains provide a playground for outdoor enthusiasts, offering opportunities for hiking, cycling, and skiing. The Mont Sainte-

Odile, a significant historical and religious site, rewards visitors with panoramic views and a glimpse into the region's past. The Unterlinden Museum in Colmar houses the Isenheim Altarpiece, a masterpiece of Renaissance art, among other notable works.

Southern Alsace

Southern Alsace is a captivating blend of history, culture, and breathtaking natural beauty. Encompassing the departments of Haut-Rhin and Bas-Rhin within the Grand Est region, Southern Alsace is renowned for its idyllic villages, sprawling vineyards, and the imposing Vosges Mountains that define its landscape. This enchanting region offers a wealth of experiences for visitors seeking to immerse themselves in its rich heritage and diverse charms.

Geography: Southern Alsace's geography is a fascinating mosaic of contrasts, ranging from the fertile plains of the Rhine Valley to the rugged terrain of the Vosges Mountains. The region's eastern border is delineated by the Rhine River, a natural boundary that also marks the frontier with Germany. To the south, Southern Alsace shares a border with Switzerland, creating a unique cultural crossroads where French, German, and Swiss influences converge. The Ill River, a tributary of the Rhine, meanders through the region, nurturing the land and contributing to its agricultural prosperity.

The Vosges Mountains, a dominant feature of the landscape, offer a haven for outdoor enthusiasts. Their dense forests, pristine lakes, and cascading waterfalls beckon hikers, nature lovers, and adventurers. The Grand Ballon, the highest peak in the southern Vosges, stands as a majestic sentinel, offering panoramic views of the surrounding valleys and plains. As the mountains gradually descend towards the east, they give way to the gentle slopes and fertile plains that are synonymous with Alsace's world-renowned vineyards and orchards.

Climate: Southern Alsace experiences a semi-continental climate, characterized by warm summers and cold winters. The region benefits from a relatively low annual precipitation, with an average rainfall of 500 to 700 millimeters. This climate, combined with the region's fertile soils, creates ideal conditions for viticulture, making Alsace one of France's premier wine-producing regions. The vineyards of Southern Alsace thrive in the abundant sunshine and cool nights, producing a wide array of celebrated white wines, including Riesling, Gewürztraminer, and Pinot Blanc.

Historical Legacy: The history of Southern Alsace is woven with threads from diverse cultures and civilizations. Evidence of early human settlements dates back to the Paleolithic era, attesting to the region's ancient roots. During the Roman period, Alsace played a significant role as a part of the Roman Empire, and remnants of Roman architecture can still be found throughout the region.

The Middle Ages saw Alsace become a coveted territory, contested by the Holy Roman Empire and the Kingdom of France. The region's strategic location along the Rhine River made it a valuable asset, and control over Alsace shifted back and forth between the two powers. The Treaty of Westphalia in 1648, which marked the end of the Thirty Years' War, solidified French control over Alsace, although the region continued to experience cultural and political shifts in the centuries that followed.

The 19th and 20th centuries were a time of upheaval for Alsace, as it was annexed by Germany following the Franco-Prussian War in 1871 and then returned to France after World War I. The region once again endured German occupation during World War II before being liberated by Allied forces in 1945. Today, Alsace remains an integral part of France, enriched by its complex history and multicultural heritage.

Cultural Fusion: The culture of Southern Alsace is a unique blend of French and German influences, a result of its historical and geographical context. This cultural fusion is evident in the region's architecture, cuisine, traditions, and even its language. The half-timbered houses that grace the villages of Alsace are reminiscent of Germanic architectural styles, while the French influence is reflected in the language spoken by the locals and the culinary traditions that have been passed down through generations.

Alsatian cuisine is a testament to the region's cultural diversity, offering a delectable fusion of French and German flavors. Hearty dishes like choucroute garnie, tarte flambée, and baeckeoffe are staples of the local culinary scene, while the region's pastries, such as kougelhopf and bredele, are renowned for their exquisite taste and craftsmanship.

Flora and Fauna: The diverse landscapes of Southern Alsace support a rich array of flora and fauna. The forests of the Vosges Mountains provide a habitat for a variety of wildlife, including red deer, wild boar, and lynx. Birdwatchers will be delighted by the abundance of avian species, such as the black woodpecker, peregrine falcon, and capercaillie.

The plains and vineyards of Alsace are dotted with wildflowers, creating different colors in spring and summer. Orchids, gentians, and anemones are just a few of the many floral species that thrive in the region's fertile soils. The Rhine River and its tributaries are home to a variety of fish, amphibians, and aquatic plants, adding to the ecological diversity of the area.

Best Time to Visit: The ideal time to visit Southern Alsace depends on your personal preferences and interests. Spring and summer are perfect for outdoor enthusiasts, offering opportunities for hiking, cycling, and exploring the vineyards in bloom. The mild weather and scenic landscapes make this a wonderful time to experience the region's natural beauty.

Autumn, with its vibrant foliage and the excitement of the grape harvest, is a particularly enchanting time to visit. Wine festivals and tastings abound, providing a unique insight into the region's winemaking traditions. Winter transforms Alsace into a magical wonderland, with charming Christmas markets, festive decorations, and opportunities for skiing and snowboarding in the Vosges Mountains.

Travel Logistics: Southern Alsace is well-connected to major cities in France and neighboring countries, making it easily accessible for travelers. The region's main cities, such as Mulhouse and Colmar, are served by train connections from Paris, Strasbourg, and other major hubs. The EuroAirport Basel-Mulhouse-Freiburg, located in the tri-national region of France, Switzerland, and Germany, serves as a major international gateway to Southern Alsace.

Within the region, an efficient network of buses and trains connects towns and villages, making it easy to get around without a car. However, renting a car is a convenient option for those who wish to explore the countryside at their own pace and discover hidden gems off the beaten path.

Notable Towns and Villages: Southern Alsace is dotted with charming towns and villages, each with its own unique character and history. Colmar, the "capital of Alsatian wine," enchants visitors with its well-preserved medieval architecture, vibrant flower displays, and picturesque canals. Eguisheim, with its concentric layout and colorful half-timbered houses, exudes a timeless charm and offers a glimpse into the region's winemaking traditions. Riquewihr, a fortified village surrounded by vineyards, transports visitors back to the Middle Ages with its cobblestone streets, historic buildings, and panoramic views of the Vosges Mountains.

Natural Reserves and Landmarks: Southern Alsace is home to a number of natural reserves and landmarks that showcase the region's natural beauty and cultural heritage. The Ballons des Vosges Regional Nature Park, a vast protected area that encompasses the highest peaks of the Vosges Mountains, is a paradise for outdoor enthusiasts. Hiking trails wind through forests and meadows, leading to stunning viewpoints and hidden waterfalls. The park is also home to a diverse range of flora and fauna, making it a haven for nature lovers.

The Haut-Koenigsbourg Castle, a medieval fortress perched on a hilltop overlooking the Alsatian plain, is a testament to the region's rich history. Meticulously restored to its former glory, the castle offers visitors a chance to step back in time and explore its towers, ramparts, and gardens while enjoying panoramic views of the surrounding landscape.

Outdoor Activities: Southern Alsace is a playground for outdoor enthusiasts, with a wide range of activities to suit all interests and skill levels. Hiking is a popular pastime, with countless trails that traverse the Vosges Mountains and the scenic vineyards. The GR5 long-distance trail, which passes through the region, offers a challenging yet rewarding adventure for experienced hikers.

Cycling is another great way to explore the region's diverse landscapes. The Alsace Wine Route, a dedicated cycling route that stretches for over 170 kilometers, takes riders through charming villages, rolling vineyards, and historic sites. Along the way, cyclists can stop to sample local wines and cuisine, adding to the enjoyment of the journey.

Water sports enthusiasts can take to the Rhine River and its tributaries for kayaking, canoeing, and fishing. The region's lakes and reservoirs offer opportunities for swimming, boating, and other water-based activities.

Stargazing: The pristine skies of Southern Alsace, particularly in the Vosges Mountains, make it an ideal destination for stargazing. The Ballons des Vosges Regional Nature Park, designated as a Dark Sky Reserve, offers exceptional conditions for observing the night sky. Visitors can marvel at the Milky Way, constellations, and other celestial phenomena, away from the Light pollution of urban areas. The park organizes stargazing events and workshops, providing a unique opportunity to learn about astronomy and appreciate the wonders of the cosmos.

Top Cities and Towns

Strasbourg

Strasbourg, a city of captivating contrasts, is the beating heart of France's Grand Est region. Its location on the border with Germany has imbued it with a unique cultural identity, a dynamic fusion of French and German influences that permeates its architecture, cuisine, and traditions. Steeped in history, Strasbourg boasts a legacy that stretches back centuries, evident in its well-preserved medieval architecture and its pivotal role in European politics.

History: Strasbourg's strategic location, nestled on the banks of the Ill and Rhine rivers, has made it a coveted prize throughout history. Its name, derived from the German words "Strass" (street) and "Burg" (city), reflects its importance as a crossroads in medieval trade routes. The city's past is marked by its alternating allegiance between France and Germany, a testament to its strategic significance and the complex historical forces that have shaped its identity.

Geographical Setting and Climate: Strasbourg's geographic location at the confluence of the Ill and Rhine rivers has played a pivotal role in its development as a major trade and cultural center. Its temperate climate, with warm summers and cold winters, creates a pleasant environment for residents and visitors alike. The city's proximity to the Rhine River has also contributed to its economic prosperity, facilitating trade and transportation throughout history.

Architectural Heritage: The architectural landscape of Strasbourg is a testament to its rich historical legacy. The Strasbourg Cathedral, an awe-inspiring Gothic masterpiece, stands as a symbol of the city's medieval grandeur. For over two centuries, it held the title of the tallest building in the world, and it remains the highest structure built entirely during the medieval period. The cathedral's intricate facade, adorned with sculptures and delicate details, is a testament to the craftsmanship of its time. The interior, with its soaring vaults and stained-glass windows, evokes a sense of reverence and wonder.

Petite France: The district of Petite France, with its charming black and white half-timbered houses and meandering cobblestone streets, transports visitors to a bygone era. Once home to millers, fishermen, and tanners, this picturesque quarter now offers a glimpse into Strasbourg's traditional Alsatian way of life. Visitors can wander through its narrow lanes, admire the quaint architecture, and savor the flavors of authentic Alsatian cuisine.

Cultural Fusion: Strasbourg's cultural identity is a unique blend of French and German influences. The city's language, cuisine, and traditions reflect this cultural fusion. Alsatian, the local dialect, combines elements of both French and German, creating a linguistic tapestry that is as diverse as the region itself. The city's culinary scene is equally eclectic, with dishes like choucroute garnie (sauerkraut with sausages and meats) and kugelhopf cake (a sweet yeast cake) showcasing the harmonious blend of French and German flavors.

A European Capital: Strasbourg's significance extends beyond its national borders. As the official seat of the European Parliament, it plays a pivotal role in the European Union. The city also houses the Council of Europe and the European Court of Human Rights, making it a hub for international diplomacy and cooperation. This international presence contributes to Strasbourg's cosmopolitan atmosphere, attracting visitors from all corners of the globe.

Green Spaces and Sustainability: Strasbourg's commitment to environmental sustainability is evident in its abundance of green spaces. The Parc de l'Orangerie, one of the city's most beloved parks, offers a tranquil oasis in the heart of the urban landscape. With its picturesque boating lake, long avenues shaded by leafy trees, and a charming mini-zoo, the park provides a welcome escape for residents and visitors alike.

Festive Celebrations: Throughout the year, Strasbourg comes alive with a myriad of cultural events and festivals that celebrate its heritage and the arts. Music and film festivals showcase local and international talent, while the city's renowned Christmas markets create a magical atmosphere during the holiday season. These festive events, along with countless others, contribute to Strasbourg's vibrant cultural scene and offer visitors a unique opportunity to experience the city's joie de vivre.

Education and Innovation: Strasbourg is a city that values knowledge and innovation. It is home to the prestigious University of Strasbourg, a renowned institution of higher education, as well as several other universities and research centers. This focus on education and research fosters a dynamic intellectual environment, attracting students and scholars from around the world.

Colmar

Colmar, a jewel in the crown of northeastern France, is a city steeped in history and bursting with charm. Often referred to as the "most Alsatian city of Alsace," Colmar encapsulates the essence of the region's rich heritage, vibrant culture, and picturesque landscapes. Its quaint cobblestone streets, colorful half-timbered houses, and tranquil canals transport visitors to a bygone era, while its culinary delights, artistic treasures, and festive celebrations offer a taste of the region's unique joie de vivre.

A Glimpse into the Past: Colmar's history dates back over a millennium, with its first documented mention occurring in 823. During the High Middle Ages, Colmar flourished as a member of the Decapolis, a league of ten free imperial cities within the Holy Roman Empire. Its strategic location along major trade routes contributed to its economic prosperity, particularly in the wine trade, which played a pivotal role in shaping the city's identity.

Architectural Heritage: Colmar's architectural landscape is a testament to its rich and diverse past. The city's old town, meticulously preserved, is a labyrinth of narrow streets lined with half-timbered houses that date back to the Renaissance and medieval periods. The Pfister House, a remarkable example of Renaissance architecture, stands as an iconic symbol of the city's past. The Saint Martin Church, a Gothic masterpiece constructed between 1235 and 1365, further enriches Colmar's architectural tapestry, showcasing the region's religious heritage.

Little Venice: A Tranquil Oasis: At the heart of Colmar's allure lies the enchanting district of Little Venice. This picturesque quarter, named for its network of canals and charming bridges, is a haven of tranquility and beauty. Half-timbered houses, many of which date back to the 14th and 18th centuries, line the canals, their colorful facades reflected in the water. A boat ride through these waterways offers a unique perspective of the city's architectural treasures and allows visitors to experience the serene atmosphere of this unique district.

Cultural Legacy: Colmar's cultural heritage is as rich and diverse as its architecture. The city is the birthplace of Frédéric Auguste Bartholdi, the sculptor who created the iconic Statue of Liberty.

The Bartholdi Museum, housed in the artist's former family home, celebrates his life and work, offering visitors a glimpse into the creative process behind one of the world's most recognizable monuments. The Unterlinden Museum, a renowned art institution, houses a vast collection that includes the Isenheim Altarpiece, a masterpiece of German Renaissance art that is considered one of the museum's most prized possessions.

Culinary Delights: Colmar's culinary scene is a testament to its Alsatian heritage, blending French and German culinary traditions to create a unique and flavorful experience. Tarte flambée, a thin-crust pizza-like dish topped with crème fraîche, onions, and bacon, is a beloved local specialty. Coq au Riesling, chicken cooked in a Riesling wine sauce, is another must-try dish that showcases the region's love for wine. The city's covered market is a bustling hub of activity, offering a wide array of local produce, cheeses, pastries, and other culinary delights.

Festivals and Events: Throughout the year, Colmar hosts a vibrant array of festivals and events that celebrate its culture, traditions, and artistic spirit. The Colmar International Festival, a prestigious music festival, attracts renowned musicians and performers from around the world. The city's Christmas markets, renowned for their enchanting atmosphere and festive spirit, transform Colmar into a winter wonderland during the holiday season.

Natural Splendor: Colmar's location amidst the vineyards of Alsace, with the Vosges Mountains and the Rhine River as a backdrop, provides ample opportunities to connect with nature. The nearby wine route, winding through picturesque villages and rolling vineyards, offers a scenic escape into the heart of the Alsatian countryside. Visitors can indulge in wine tastings, vineyard tours, and breathtaking views of the surrounding landscape.

Mulhouse

Mulhouse, a city nestled in the heart of the Haut-Rhin department in France, stands as a testament to the nation's rich industrial heritage and a vibrant cultural landscape. As the largest city in the department and the second largest in the Alsace region after Strasbourg, Mulhouse boasts a unique identity that blends its historical roots as a textile powerhouse with a modern outlook focused on innovation and cultural diversity.

Industrial Heritage: Mulhouse's history is deeply intertwined with the textile industry, which emerged in the mid-18th century and propelled the city to the forefront of France's industrial landscape. The Koechlin family, pioneers in cotton cloth manufacturing, played a pivotal role in establishing Mulhouse as a leading textile center in the 19th century. This industrial prowess earned Mulhouse the moniker "the French Manchester," a testament to its economic significance and the scale of its textile production. The city's factories, once bustling with activity, now serve as reminders of its industrious past, their architectural grandeur a testament to the ambition and innovation of the era.

Cultural Melting Pot: Beyond its industrial legacy, Mulhouse is a city with a rich and diverse cultural heritage. Its unique history, marked by a period of independence until 1798 and close ties with Swiss cantons, has shaped its distinct identity. The city's historical center, a labyrinth of charming alleys and architectural wonders, reflects this unique blend of influences. Mulhouse's cultural scene is a vibrant tapestry, woven together by the contributions of its diverse communities.

Museums and Attractions: Mulhouse's reputation as a city of museums is well-deserved. The Cité de l'Automobile, home to the largest automobile collection in the world, is a mecca for car enthusiasts, showcasing a breathtaking array of vintage and modern vehicles. The Cité du Train, Europe's largest railway museum, offers a fascinating journey through the history of rail transportation, with exhibits that range from steam locomotives to high-speed trains. These museums, along with others dedicated to art, history, and science, provide visitors with a comprehensive and engaging look into Mulhouse's past, present, and future.

Festivals and Events: The cultural calendar of Mulhouse consist of different events that celebrate the city's diverse heritage and creative spirit. From the lively Chipo'zik concert to the passionate Tango festival and the festive Journées d'Octobre, Mulhouse offers a wide array of cultural experiences that cater to all interests. These events, often held in the city's historic squares and parks, bring the community together and provide a platform for artists and performers to showcase their talents.

Natural Splendor: Mulhouse's urban landscape is complemented by the natural beauty of its surroundings. The Vosges Mountains, with their lush forests and scenic trails, offer a serene escape from the city's hustle and bustle. The Rhine River, a lifeline for the region, provides opportunities for leisurely walks, boat rides, and moments of quiet reflection. The city's proximity to these natural wonders allows residents and visitors to easily transition from urban exploration to outdoor adventures, creating a well-rounded and enriching experience.

Modern Developments: Mulhouse is a city that embraces innovation and progress. Its commitment to education and research is evident in the presence of institutions like the Upper Alsace University, which plays a crucial role in fostering intellectual growth and technological advancement. The city's ongoing development projects, from urban renewal initiatives to the creation of new cultural spaces, demonstrate its dynamism and adaptability. Mulhouse is a city that is constantly evolving, striving to create a better future for its residents and visitors alike.

Obernai

Obernai stands as a captivating testament to the region's rich history and enduring traditions. With roots tracing back to the Roman era, this charming town exudes a timeless allure, where the echoes of the past reverberate through its cobblestone streets and half-timbered houses. Obernai is a place where history is not merely confined to museums and monuments; it is woven into the very fabric of daily life, shaping the town's architecture, customs, and culinary traditions.

A Journey Through Time: Obernai's historical significance dates back to the Roman period, when it served as a vital crossroads, facilitating trade and cultural exchange. In subsequent centuries, the town evolved into a Merovingian royal villa, a testament to its importance in the region's political landscape. The earliest recorded mention of Obernai, then known as Ehenheim, appears in historical documents in 778. The town's name would later change to Oberehnheim in 1242, distinguishing it from the nearby village of Niederehnheim (Niedernai).

Obernai's transformation into a town around 1240, under the patronage of the Hohenstaufen family, marked a pivotal moment in its history. The town's burgeoning viticulture and flourishing craft industries fueled its growth and prosperity, culminating in its admission to the Décapole in 1354, an alliance of ten imperial towns in Alsace that enjoyed significant autonomy and privileges within the Holy Roman Empire.

Cultural Heritage and Reverence for Sainte-Odile: Obernai's cultural heritage is deeply intertwined with the legacy of Sainte-

Odile, the patron saint of Alsace. Born blind, Sainte-Odile miraculously regained her sight upon being baptized at the tender age of thirteen. This miraculous event is commemorated throughout the region, and Obernai holds a special connection to the saint, with numerous landmarks and traditions dedicated to her memory. The town's architectural landscape reflects this rich cultural tapestry, with buildings from the Renaissance period, such as the Town Hall and the Corn Market, standing as proud symbols of Obernai's past.

Architectural Splendor and Historical Landmarks: A stroll through Obernai's well-preserved medieval center is akin to stepping back in time. The town's cobblestone streets, lined with half-timbered houses adorned with intricate woodwork and colorful flower boxes, exude a timeless charm. The Château de Guirbaden and Château du Spesbourg, perched on hilltops overlooking the town, offer a glimpse into the region's feudal history, their imposing ruins evoking tales of knights, chivalry, and courtly intrigue. The town's medieval fortifications, towers, and the Puits à Six Seaux, a well dating back to 1579, are further testaments to Obernai's rich historical legacy.

Festive Celebrations and Community Spirit: Obernai's vibrant community spirit is reflected in its diverse calendar of festivals and events. The Festival de Musique d'Obernai, a celebration of classical and contemporary music, showcases the town's artistic vibrancy and commitment to cultural expression. Other notable events include the Obernai-Benfeld International Triathlon, a challenging athletic competition, and the International Organ Festival, which highlights the town's musical heritage. The Pedestrian race - Les O'nze kms d'Obernai is a popular event that attracts runners from far and wide, showcasing the town's scenic beauty and welcoming atmosphere.

Gastronomic Traditions: Obernai's culinary traditions are as unique as its history. Unlike the typical red skirt and black headdress commonly associated with Alsatian attire, the traditional dress worn by Obernai women draws inspiration from the outfit worn by Queen Marie Antoinette when she dressed as a shepherdess for country fairs at Versailles. This historical connection is evident in the town's cuisine, which features a refined and elegant style, with bright floral and pastel-colored silk skirts and delicate aprons adding a touch of sophistication to the culinary experience.

A Thriving Modern Town: While Obernai cherishes its historical roots, it has also embraced modernity, evolving into an important hub for employment and tourism. Over the past two decades, the town's population has doubled, a testament to its growing appeal as a place to live and visit. Obernai's commitment to preserving its heritage while adapting to the needs of the 21st century has created a unique blend of old-world charm and contemporary vibrancy.

Riquewihr

Riquewihr, a captivating commune nestled in the Haut-Rhin department of the Grand Est region in northeastern France, is a living testament to the enduring charm of Alsatian heritage and history. With its meticulously preserved medieval architecture and its vibrant cultural traditions, Riquewihr is a destination that beckons travelers to step back in time and immerse themselves in a world of enchantment and wonder.

History: The story of Riquewihr is a captivating narrative that unfolds over centuries, marked by periods of prosperity, resilience, and unwavering dedication to its cultural roots. The village's origins trace back to approximately 800 AD when a Frankish landowner named Richo established an estate in the area, thus giving rise to the name "Richovilla," the precursor to Riquewihr's present-day moniker. By 1094, Riquewihr had already established itself as a center for viticulture, cultivating the grapes that would eventually contribute to its renowned winemaking tradition. In 1291, the town fortified itself with sturdy walls and a protective moat, a testament to the strategic importance of its location. By the 16th century, Riquewihr had risen to prominence as the capital of the Württemberg lands in Alsace, a testament to its economic and political significance.

A Rich Cultural Heritage: Riquewihr's cultural identity is inextricably linked to its winemaking heritage. For centuries, the village served as a Winzerdorf, or "wine village," functioning as a bustling hub for the trade of Alsatian and German wines. This viticultural legacy continues to thrive today, with Riquewihr proudly positioned along the celebrated Alsace Wine Route. The village's wine cellars, with their vaulted ceilings and centuries-old barrels, offer a glimpse into the heart of this cherished tradition.

Architectural Splendor: A stroll through Riquewihr is akin to stepping into a living museum of Renaissance architecture. The village's meticulously preserved half-timbered houses, adorned with intricate carvings and colorful facades, stand as a testament to the craftsmanship and artistry of a bygone era. Ornate fountains, weathered wells, and winding cobblestone streets contribute to the village's timeless charm. The Dolder, a 13th-century defensive gate, and the Thieves' Tower, a reminder of the village's medieval past, are iconic landmarks that add to Riquewihr's historical allure.

Modern-Day Allure: Today, Riquewihr continues to captivate visitors with its well-preserved medieval fortifications and its enchanting atmosphere. The village is overlooked by a majestic castle that dates back to the same period, now transformed into a museum that offers insights into the region's history and culture. Riquewihr's exceptional beauty and historical significance have earned it a coveted place among the "Les Plus Beaux Villages de France" (The Most Beautiful Villages of France), a testament to its enduring appeal.

Festive Celebrations: Riquewihr's calendar is punctuated by a vibrant array of festivals and events that celebrate its rich heritage and cultural traditions. Wine festivals, gastronomic walks, and other festive gatherings fill the village with joyous energy throughout the year. These events often feature wine tastings, folk music performances, and lively demonstrations of traditional crafts, creating an atmosphere of warmth and conviviality.

Gastronomic Delights: The culinary landscape of Riquewihr is a reflection of its cultural influences, seamlessly blending French and German culinary traditions. Visitors can savor local specialties such as tarte flambée, a savory flatbread topped with crème fraîche, onions, and bacon, and coq au Riesling, a succulent chicken dish cooked in a Riesling wine sauce. The village's renowned Riesling wines, celebrated for their crisp acidity and complex aromas, perfectly complement the local cuisine.

Cultural Attractions

Museums and Galleries

In the heart of Strasbourg, the Contemporary and Modern Art Museum stands as a beacon for art enthusiasts. Its collection spans a wide range of artistic movements and styles, providing a comprehensive overview of modern and contemporary art. The museum's thoughtfully curated exhibitions invite visitors to engage with thought-provoking works that challenge and inspire.

Also in Strasbourg, the Musée des Beaux-Arts, housed within the opulent Palais Rohan, is a treasure trove of old master paintings. Its collection spans from the 14th century to 1871, showcasing the works of both Upper Rhenish and non-Upper Rhenish artists. The museum offers a fascinating glimpse into the artistic heritage of the region and its connections to broader European artistic traditions.

The Musée Adolf Michaelis, another gem in Strasbourg, transports visitors to the ancient world. Its collection, amassed by Adolf Michaelis in the 19th century, features artifacts from ancient Egypt, the Middle East, Greece, and Rome. The museum's photographic archive, documenting archaeological excavations, further enriches the experience, providing a visual record of the discoveries that have shaped our understanding of ancient civilizations.

The Musée de Marmoutier, housed in a beautifully preserved house dating back to 1590, offers a unique perspective on the region's history and culture. Its collection of Judaica is among the most significant in the area, shedding light on the Jewish community's contributions to Alsatian society. The museum also provides insights into rural life in Alsace during the 18th and 19th centuries, showcasing tools, household items, and other artifacts that illuminate the daily lives of the region's inhabitants.

Colmar, another cultural hub in Alsace, is home to the renowned Musée Unterlinden. This museum boasts a vast collection that spans centuries, encompassing a wide range of artistic styles and movements. However, its most celebrated treasure is undoubtedly the Isenheim Altarpiece, a masterpiece of German Renaissance art that draws visitors from around the world.

In Wingen-sur-Moder, the Lalique Museum pays homage to the life and work of René Lalique, a visionary artist and designer who revolutionized the world of glassmaking and jewelry. The museum's exhibits trace the evolution of Lalique's creations, from his early Art Nouveau designs to his later Art Deco masterpieces, showcasing his exceptional craftsmanship and innovative spirit.

Back in Strasbourg, the Musée de l'Œuvre Notre-Dame focuses on Upper Rhenish art from the Middle Ages to the Renaissance. Its collection includes a wealth of sculptures, stained glass, and architectural fragments that offer a glimpse into the artistic and religious practices of the region during this pivotal period.

The Musee Bartholdi in Colmar celebrates the life and work of Auguste Bartholdi, the sculptor who gifted the world the iconic Statue of Liberty. Housed in Bartholdi's former family home, the museum showcases his sculptures, drawings, and personal belongings, providing a unique insight into the artist's creative process and the inspiration behind his most famous creation.

For those seeking a more contemporary artistic experience, the Musée d'Art Moderne et Contemporain in Strasbourg is a must-visit. Its collection spans a wide range of modern and contemporary art, including works by local artists who have made significant contributions to the art world. The museum's well-designed spaces and thought-provoking exhibitions create an engaging and immersive experience for visitors.

The Musée Würth in Erstein offers another perspective on modern and contemporary art. Its exhibitions often delve into themes of history and society, encouraging visitors to reflect on the complex interplay between art and the world around them.

In Strasbourg, the Musée Tomi Ungerer - Centre international de l'Illustration pays tribute to the renowned illustrator Tomi Ungerer. The museum's vast collection of illustrations, covering a wide array of themes and subjects, showcases Ungerer's wit, satire, and social commentary.

The Village of Hansi and his Museum in Colmar is dedicated to the artist Jean-Jacques Waltz, better known as Hansi. His works, characterized by their patriotic themes and depictions of Alsatian life, offer a glimpse into the region's cultural identity and historical struggles.

For those seeking a more unconventional experience, the Château Musée Vodou in Strasbourg offers a fascinating exploration of Vodou religious art and artifacts. The museum's collection provides a unique perspective on spiritual practices and cultural traditions from around the world.

Finally, the Musée des Arts Décoratifs de Strasbourg, located in the Palais Rohan, showcases decorative arts from the Middle Ages to the 19th century. Its collection includes furniture, ceramics, textiles, and other objects that reflect the artistic and social trends of the time.

The museums and galleries of Alsace offer a diverse and enriching cultural experience, inviting visitors to explore the region's rich history, artistic traditions, and contemporary perspectives.

Historic Sites

Castles and Fortifications: One of the most iconic landmarks in Alsace is the Château du Haut-Koenigsbourg. Situated high in the Vosges Mountains, this imposing castle offers panoramic views of the surrounding landscape and a fascinating journey back to the Middle Ages. Its towers, ramparts, and chambers have witnessed centuries of history, from medieval battles to aristocratic life.

The Château du Morimont, dating back to the 13th century, is another architectural marvel that reflects the region's turbulent past. Its design showcases the transition from a medieval fortress to a Renaissance residence, with elements of both styles evident in its structure and layout.

Fleckenstein Castle, nestled in the Northern Vosges Regional Nature Park, is a remarkable example of a rock castle. Built directly into the sandstone cliffs, it exemplifies the ingenuity of medieval architects and offers a unique perspective on the region's defensive strategies.

Medieval Towns and Villages: Colmar, with its well-preserved old town and picturesque canals, is a living museum of medieval and Renaissance architecture. Its colorful half-timbered houses, adorned with flower boxes and intricate carvings, create a postcard-perfect scene that transports visitors back in time.

Riquewihr, another gem of Alsace, has retained its medieval charm remarkably well. Its narrow streets, lined with half-timbered houses and shops selling local crafts and produce, exude an atmosphere of tranquility and authenticity. The village's 16th-century fortifications and defensive towers stand as a reminder of its strategic importance in the past.

Obernai, with its impressive fortifications and historical buildings, is a testament to the region's prosperity during the Middle Ages. Its imposing ramparts, watchtowers, and gates offer a glimpse into the town's defensive strategies, while its well-preserved houses and squares showcase the architectural styles of the era.

Religious Heritage: The Strasbourg Cathedral, a masterpiece of Gothic architecture, dominates the skyline of Strasbourg and serves as a symbol of the city's religious and cultural heritage. Its intricate facade, adorned with sculptures and statues, is a testament to the skill and artistry of medieval craftsmen. The cathedral's astronomical clock, a marvel of engineering, continues to draw crowds with its hourly displays of moving figures and celestial calculations.

Mont Sainte-Odile, a prominent hill in the Vosges Mountains, is a site of great spiritual significance. Its monastery, founded by Saint Odile in the 7th century, is a place of pilgrimage and contemplation. The hill offers breathtaking views of the surrounding landscape and is steeped in legends and historical events.

Cultural and Historical Landmarks: Neuf-Brisach, a fortified town designed by the renowned military engineer Vauban, is a UNESCO World Heritage site. Its unique star-shaped layout and elaborate system of fortifications offer a fascinating insight into 17th-century military architecture.

The Humanist Library in Sélestat houses a remarkable collection of medieval manuscripts and early printed books. It stands as a testament to the intellectual and cultural flourishing of the Renaissance period in Alsace.

Places of Remembrance: Alsace also bears witness to the tragedies of war. Hartmannswillerkopf, a national monument, commemorates the fierce battles fought in the Vosges Mountains during World War I. The European Centre of Deported Resistance Members, located in Natzweiler-Struthof, honors the memory of resistance fighters who were deported and imprisoned in the concentration camp during World War II.

Architectural Gems: La Petite France, a historic quarter in Strasbourg, is a UNESCO World Heritage site that captivates visitors with its half-timbered houses, narrow canals, and picturesque bridges. The Grande Île, the historic heart of Strasbourg, is another architectural gem, featuring a harmonious blend of medieval and Renaissance buildings.

Museums and Living History: The Ecomusée d'Alsace, an open-air museum, offers a unique opportunity to step back in time and experience traditional Alsatian rural life. Visitors can explore authentic houses, workshops, and farmsteads, gaining insights into the region's agricultural heritage and daily life in centuries past.

The Cité de l'Automobile in Mulhouse boasts the largest collection of automobiles in the world, showcasing a vast array of vintage and modern vehicles that tell the story of automotive innovation and design.

Religious Landmarks

Strasbourg Cathedral: At the heart of Strasbourg, the Cathédrale Notre Dame de Strasbourg stands as a magnificent example of Gothic architecture. Its intricate facade, adorned with countless sculptures and intricate details, is a testament to the skill and artistry of medieval craftsmen. The cathedral's astronomical clock, a marvel of engineering and artistry, continues to fascinate visitors with its complex mechanisms and celestial displays. Ascend the cathedral's spire, once the tallest in the world, to be rewarded with panoramic views of the city and the surrounding countryside.

Mont Sainte-Odile Abbey: Nestled atop the Vosges Mountains, Mont Sainte-Odile Abbey exudes an aura of tranquility and spiritual reverence. Dedicated to Saint Odile, the patron saint of Alsace, the abbey has been a place of pilgrimage and contemplation for centuries. The surrounding landscape, dotted with vineyards and forests, offers a serene backdrop for spiritual reflection. The abbey's most intriguing feature is the Pagan Wall, an ancient stone wall that encircles the hilltop. Its origins remain shrouded in mystery, adding to the allure of this sacred site.

Eglise Saint-Martin in Colmar: In the heart of Colmar, the Eglise Saint-Martin, or St. Martin's Church, stands as a testament to the architectural grandeur of the Middle Ages. Its imposing Gothic structure, with its soaring ceilings, intricate stonework, and vibrant stained glass windows, evokes a sense of awe and reverence. The church's interior is adorned with religious artwork that reflects the spiritual devotion of the time, offering visitors a glimpse into the artistic and religious traditions of the region.

Chapelle Saint-Léon IX in Eguisheim: The Chapelle Saint-Léon IX, located in the picturesque village of Eguisheim, is a stunning example of neo-Romanesque architecture. Dedicated to Pope Saint Léon IX, a native of Alsace, the chapel features beautiful stained-glass windows depicting the Saints of Alsace and paintings that illustrate scenes from the life of Saint Léon. The chapel's serene atmosphere and exquisite craftsmanship make it a place of quiet reflection and spiritual inspiration.

Eglise des Dominicains in Colmar: Another architectural gem in Colmar, the Eglise des Dominicains, is a Gothic church renowned for its magnificent altarpiece by Martin Schongauer. This masterpiece depicts the Virgin Mary with Jesus and is considered one of the most important works of religious art in the region. The church's high, vaulted ceilings and tranquil ambiance create a space that is both majestic and serene, inviting contemplation and prayer.

Église Saint-Pierre-le-Jeune in Strasbourg: The Église Saint-Pierre-le-Jeune, located in Strasbourg, boasts a unique blend of Romanesque and Gothic architectural elements. Its origins date back to the 7th century, making it one of the oldest churches in the region. The church's interior is adorned with beautiful frescoes and intricate stone carvings, while its historical significance as a key religious site throughout Alsace's history adds to its allure.

Église Saint-Thomas in Strasbourg: Often referred to as the "Protestant Cathedral" of Strasbourg, the Église Saint-Thomas is a significant landmark for the Lutheran faith. Its grand organ, built by the renowned organ builder Johann Andreas Silbermann, is celebrated for its rich and powerful sound. The church also houses the mausoleum of Marshal Maurice de Saxe, a renowned military leader.

Notre-Dame du Bischenberg in Bischoffsheim: The Notre-Dame du Bischenberg sanctuary, located in Bischoffsheim, is a place of pilgrimage and reflection for those seeking spiritual solace. Its peaceful setting, amidst the rolling hills of Alsace, provides a serene environment for prayer and contemplation. The sanctuary's history and traditions make it a significant site for both locals and visitors seeking a deeper connection to their faith.

The Humanist Library in Sélestat: While not a religious site in the traditional sense, the Humanist Library in Sélestat holds a wealth of religious manuscripts and early printed books that offer insights into the intellectual and spiritual life of the Renaissance period in Alsace. Its collection, a testament to the region's rich scholarly heritage, includes rare and valuable texts that shed light on the religious and philosophical debates of the time.

The Unterlinden Museum in Colmar: The Unterlinden Museum, housed in a former convent in Colmar, is home to the Issenheim Altarpiece, a masterpiece of religious art that continues to captivate and inspire visitors. This emotionally charged work, depicting scenes from the life of Christ and the Virgin Mary, is a powerful testament to the role of art in conveying spiritual truths.

Nature and Outdoor Activities

Hiking and Biking Trails

Hiking Trails: For hiking enthusiasts, Alsace presents a myriad of options that showcase the region's diverse terrain and scenic landscapes. The GR5 Trail, a legendary long-distance path that is part of the European E2 route, winds through the majestic Vosges Mountains. This iconic trail takes hikers through verdant forests, across picturesque mountain pastures, and into charming villages, offering breathtaking views at every turn.

The Way of Saint James, another long-distance trail, traverses the Vosges Mountains on its pilgrimage route to Compostela. This path holds both spiritual and scenic significance, allowing hikers to connect with the region's rich religious history while immersing themselves in the natural beauty of the landscape.

For those seeking a more moderate challenge, the Three Lakes Loop from Orbey is an excellent choice. This scenic hike circles three serene lakes, offering breathtaking views of the surrounding forests and mountains. The trail winds through diverse terrain, from lush meadows to dense woodlands, providing a varied and engaging experience.

Experienced hikers seeking a more demanding adventure can tackle the Hirschsteine Rocks via the Stairs Loop from Le Valtin. This challenging trail features steep ascents and rocky terrain, but the effort is rewarded with stunning views of the unique rock formations that characterize the area.

The Grand Ballon, the highest peak in the Vosges Mountains, is another popular destination for hikers seeking panoramic views and a sense of accomplishment. The trail to the summit is moderately challenging, but the breathtaking vistas from the top make it well worth the effort.

Biking Trails: Alsace's cycling routes are equally diverse, catering to both leisurely riders and avid cyclists. The Alsace Wine Route, a renowned cycling path, winds its way through the region's picturesque vineyards. This scenic route offers cyclists the opportunity to explore charming wine-producing villages, sample local wines, and soak in the beauty of the surrounding countryside.

The Canal de la Bruche Bicycle Path provides a more relaxed cycling experience. This tranquil path follows a scenic canal, offering a peaceful escape from the hustle and bustle of everyday life. It's an ideal route for families or those seeking a leisurely ride amidst nature.

The Rhine Cycle Route (EuroVelo 15), part of a larger European cycle route network, traverses the Rhine River, offering a flat and accessible path for cyclists of all levels. This route provides stunning views of the river and the surrounding landscapes, making it a popular choice for both short excursions and longer journeys.

Mountain Biking Trails: For mountain biking enthusiasts, Alsace offers a thrilling array of trails that traverse the Vosges Mountains. The Vosges Mountain Bike Trails cater to a variety of skill levels, from gentle forest paths to challenging downhill tracks. These trails wind through diverse terrain, offering technical challenges, exhilarating descents, and breathtaking views.

The Ballons des Vosges Nature Park, a haven for mountain bikers, features a network of marked circuits that showcase the park's diverse landscapes. From forested slopes to open meadows, these trails provide an unforgettable mountain biking experience.

Planning Your Adventure: With over 17,000 kilometers of marked trails, Alsace offers endless possibilities for outdoor adventures. Whether you're planning a multi-day trek or a short day hike, it's important to research and choose a route that aligns with your interests and fitness level. Online resources and local tourist offices can provide valuable information on trail difficulty, length, and access points.

After the Trail: After a day of exploration and adventure, Alsace welcomes weary travelers with its renowned hospitality. Farm inns, nestled amidst the countryside, offer hearty meals and cozy accommodations. Numerous lodges and refuges are also available along the trails, providing a welcome respite for hikers and bikers seeking rest and refreshment. These establishments not only offer comfort but also provide an opportunity to connect with the local culture and savor the flavors of Alsatian cuisine.

Parks and Gardens

Parc de Wesserling: Nestled in the town of Husseren-Wesserling, the Parc de Wesserling is a unique destination that seamlessly blends history, culture, and nature. Once a thriving royal canvas factory, the park has been transformed into a multifaceted site that showcases the region's industrial heritage.

Visitors can explore remarkable gardens, a textile eco-museum that delves into the history of textile production, and spaces dedicated to artistic creation. The park's diverse offerings make it a captivating destination for those seeking to understand the interplay between industry, culture, and the natural world.

Mulhouse Zoological and Botanical Park: While primarily known for its diverse collection of animals, the Mulhouse Zoological and Botanical Park also boasts a stunning botanical garden. This harmonious blend of flora and fauna creates a unique environment where visitors can marvel at the beauty of both the animal kingdom and the plant world. The park's meticulously maintained gardens, featuring a variety of plant species and thematic displays, offer a peaceful retreat for nature enthusiasts.

Zen Gardens: Oases of Tranquility: For those seeking a moment of serenity and reflection, Alsace offers two exquisite Zen gardens that embody the principles of Japanese garden design. The Weiterswiller Zen Temple Garden, located in the village of Weiterswiller, provides a peaceful sanctuary for meditation and contemplation. Its carefully arranged rocks, raked gravel, and tranquil water features create an atmosphere of harmony and balance. The Sekitei Japanese Garden in Mulhouse is another meticulously designed space that captures the essence of Zen aesthetics. Its minimalist design, featuring carefully pruned trees, moss-covered rocks, and serene ponds, invites visitors to slow down and appreciate the simple beauty of nature.

Domains and Gardens: Horticultural Heritage: Alsace's horticultural heritage is evident in its numerous domains and gardens, each showcasing the region's passion for cultivating beauty and tranquility. The Domaine de la Léonardsau, near Obernai, boasts a magnificent park with meticulously manicured landscapes, inviting visitors to stroll along its paths and admire its diverse flora. The Stair Garden in Brumath is a unique horticultural project that combines artistry with nature, creating a visually stunning landscape that incorporates cascading terraces and vibrant plant life. The Charles de Reinach Park in Hirtzbach, another testament to the region's horticultural expertise, features a rich variety of plant species arranged in aesthetically pleasing patterns, offering a feast for the senses.

Fort Uhrich: Fort Uhrich, located in Illkirch-Graffenstaden, offers a unique blend of history and horticulture. Visitors can explore the fort's historical fortifications, a reminder of the region's military past, while also enjoying the beauty of its surrounding gardens. The juxtaposition of these two elements creates a fascinating and thought-provoking experience.

Jardins de Gaïa: The Jardins de Gaïa in Wittisheim is a unique garden dedicated to the cultivation and promotion of local medicinal plants. This garden not only showcases the rich biodiversity of the region but also serves as a community-based healthcare system, highlighting the importance of plants in traditional medicine and promoting a holistic approach to well-being.

Strasbourg Parks: Strasbourg is dotted with numerous parks that provide green oases within the urban landscape. These parks offer residents and visitors alike a place to escape the hustle and bustle of city life and reconnect with nature. From the Parc de l'Orangerie, with its picturesque lake and mini-zoo, to the Parc de la Citadelle, with its historical fortifications and panoramic views, Strasbourg's parks offer a diverse range of experiences for all to enjoy.

Jardin Medieval and Jardin de Ville: The Jardin Medieval in Chatenois, a garden that pays homage to Alsace's rich textile past, features a collection of utilitarian plants, down plants, and plants used in dyeing. This unique garden provides a glimpse into the historical relationship between the region's craft and industrial activities. The Jardin de Ville in Ribeauville, a charming garden located in the heart of the town, offers a peaceful retreat from the bustling streets, inviting visitors to relax and soak in the ambiance of this historic town.

Wine Route and Vineyards.

Wineries of Alsace: The wineries of Alsace are renowned for their exceptional white wines, which are celebrated for their unique character and exquisite flavors. The region's distinct terroir, a harmonious blend of diverse geological formations and a favorable climate, plays a pivotal role in shaping the character of Alsatian wines. The vineyards, meticulously tended by generations of passionate winegrowers, yield grapes that are transformed into wines of exceptional quality and aromatic complexity.

Les Vignobles Ruhlmann-Schutz, a family-owned vineyard in Dambach-la-Ville, is a shining example of Alsace's winemaking heritage. With vineyards that span 50 hectares, encompassing two Grand Crus and several notable terroirs, this estate produces wines that are a testament to the region's rich soils and meticulous cultivation practices. Their commitment to traditional winemaking techniques, coupled with their focus on old vines, results in wines of unparalleled finesse and character.

Domaine Barthel, situated in Bernardvillé, is another family-owned winery that has been passed down through generations. Their dedication to preserving the region's winemaking traditions is evident in their diverse range of wines, each reflecting the unique characteristics of the vineyards from which they originate. From the crisp and refreshing Riesling to the aromatic and complex Gewürztraminer, Domaine Barthel's wines offer a taste of Alsace's rich viticultural heritage.

Louis Hauller Vins d'Alsace, located in Dambach-la-Ville, is a winery that has been producing exceptional wines for over a century. Their commitment to quality and innovation is evident in their diverse range of wines, which include both classic varietals and innovative blends. Whether you're a seasoned wine connoisseur or a curious newcomer, Louis Hauller's wines are sure to delight your palate.

The Alsace Wine Route: The Alsace Wine Route is a journey through a land where wine is not just a beverage but a way of life. This scenic route, winding through nearly 119 winegrowing villages, offers visitors the opportunity to meet passionate winegrowers, explore picturesque vineyards, and sample a wide array of Alsatian wines. The route encompasses three major AOCs (Appellation d'Origine Contrôlée): Alsace AOC for white, rosé, and red wines; Alsace Grand Cru AOC for exceptional white wines produced from specific vineyards; and Crémant d'Alsace AOC for sparkling wines. With numerous wine cellars open to the public, the Alsace Wine Route is an invitation to immerse yourself in the region's rich winemaking heritage.

Breweries of Alsace: Alsace's brewing tradition dates back to the Middle Ages, and today, the region is experiencing a craft beer renaissance. Microbreweries have sprung up throughout Alsace, each with its own unique approach to brewing and a passion for creating innovative and flavorful beers.

The Bra'v Brewery, nestled amidst the vineyards, offers a picturesque setting for enjoying craft beers. Their commitment to sustainability and community engagement is evident in their diverse range of events, which include barbecues, music festivals, and other gatherings that bring people together to celebrate the joys of beer and camaraderie.

Saint-Pierre Brewery, one of the largest craft microbreweries in Alsace, is known for its wide range of beers, from classic lagers to organic and fruity brews. Their brewing workshop offers visitors the opportunity to learn about the brewing process and even create their own unique beer.

Bisaiguë Brewery, located in the heart of Kaysersberg, is a haven for beer enthusiasts. Their sophisticated range of beers, brewed in a centuries-old vaulted cellar, reflects a passion for quality and innovation. Their collaboration with a Michelin-starred chef has resulted in an exclusive beer flavored with garden-picked plants, showcasing the creativity and ingenuity of the region's brewers.

Perle Brewery, a beloved institution in Alsace, has been producing beer since 1882. Their diverse range of beers, including organic options brewed with local wine and plants, reflects their commitment to tradition and innovation. A tour of the brewery offers visitors a glimpse into the history of Perle and the secrets behind their renowned brews.

Shopping

Markets and Boutiques

Farmers Markets: Alsace's farmers markets are a testament to the region's agricultural bounty. These lively gatherings, held in towns and villages throughout Alsace, offer a sensory feast of sights, sounds, and aromas. At the Marché Couvert in Colmar, vendors proudly display their fresh produce, from plump fruits and vegetables to artisanal cheeses and cured meats. La Nouvelle Douane in Strasbourg, housed in a historic building, offers a curated selection of local delicacies, with a particular emphasis on cheeses that reflect the region's distinct terroir. The Marché du Canal Couvert, also in Strasbourg, is a bustling hub of activity, where locals and visitors mingle amongst stalls overflowing with fresh produce, flowers, and Alsatian specialties. These markets are not just places to shop; they are vibrant social gatherings that provide a glimpse into the heart of Alsatian life.

Specialty Boutiques: Alsace's specialty boutiques are a treasure trove of unique finds and artisanal crafts. In the picturesque village of Riquewihr, shops lining the cobblestone streets offer a diverse range of traditional Alsatian products, from hand-painted pottery and delicate lacework to intricately woven textiles.

Colmar's charming alleys are home to numerous artisanal shops where skilled artisans create and sell their wares. From handcrafted jewelry adorned with local gemstones to paintings that capture the essence of the Alsatian landscape, these boutiques offer a glimpse into the region's creative spirit and artistic traditions.

Antique Shops and Brocantes: For antique enthusiasts and lovers of vintage treasures, Alsace's brocantes, or flea markets, are a must-visit. Strasbourg's Antique District is a haven for collectors, with numerous shops and stalls offering a wide array of furniture, art, collectibles, and curiosities. Brocante markets, held regularly throughout the region, provide an opportunity to uncover hidden gems and unique pieces that tell stories of the past. Whether you're searching for a rare antique or simply enjoy the thrill of the hunt, Alsace's brocantes are sure to delight.

Fashion and Design Stores: Alsace's cities, particularly Strasbourg and Colmar, offer a diverse shopping landscape that caters to fashionistas and design enthusiasts. Fashion boutiques lining the streets showcase a mix of the latest trends and traditional Alsatian attire, reflecting the region's unique sense of style. Design stores offer a curated selection of home décor, ranging from modern and minimalist pieces to classic Alsatian designs that evoke the region's rich heritage. Whether you're looking for a stylish outfit or a unique piece to adorn your home, Alsace's fashion and design stores are sure to inspire.

Local Produce and Gourmet Shops: Alsace is a culinary paradise, and its gourmet shops offer a tantalizing array of local produce and delicacies. Épiceries fines, or fine food stores, are treasure troves of gourmet delights, offering a curated selection of local and international products, including artisanal cheeses, cured meats, chocolates, spices, and other culinary treasures. Wine shops, a staple in this wine-producing region, boast an extensive selection of Alsatian wines, from crisp Rieslings to aromatic Gewürztraminers, providing the perfect opportunity to sample the region's liquid gold.

Shopping Centers and Malls: For those seeking a more contemporary shopping experience, Alsace's shopping centers and malls offer a diverse mix of international brands and local retailers. Place des Halles in Strasbourg, a sprawling complex, houses a wide array of shops, from fashion boutiques and electronics stores to restaurants and cafes.

Roppenheim The Style Outlets, located just outside Strasbourg, is a haven for bargain hunters, offering designer brands at discounted prices.

Local Crafts and Souvenirs

Handcrafted Pottery: Alsace's pottery, renowned for its beauty and functionality, is a testament to the region's rich artistic legacy. The villages of Soufflenheim and Betschdorf, in particular, are celebrated for their pottery traditions, with skilled artisans crafting exquisite pieces that have been passed down through generations. These ceramic creations, often adorned with traditional Alsatian motifs such as storks, pretzels, and floral patterns, are not only visually stunning but also serve as functional works of art, adding a touch of Alsatian charm to any home.

Textiles and Linens: Alsace's history in textile production is deeply ingrained in its cultural identity. The region's artisans continue to weave this legacy into exquisite linens and fabrics that are both beautiful and durable. Tablecloths, napkins, and kitchen towels, often embellished with regional designs and patterns, are cherished souvenirs that bring a touch of Alsatian elegance to any table setting. The intricate craftsmanship and attention to detail evident in these textiles reflect the region's commitment to quality and tradition.

Wooden Toys and Decor: The artisans of Alsace, along with their counterparts in the neighboring Black Forest region of Germany, have a long-standing tradition of crafting wooden toys and Christmas decorations. These handcrafted treasures, meticulously carved and painted with vibrant colors, evoke a sense of nostalgia and whimsy. Wooden toys, from rocking horses to intricate puzzles, delight children and adults alike, while hand-painted ornaments and nativity scenes bring the warmth of Christmas spirit into homes.

Culinary Specialties: Alsace is a gastronomic paradise, and its culinary specialties are a reflection of its rich cultural heritage and fertile terroir. Local mustards, crafted with unique blends of spices and herbs, offer a burst of flavor to any dish. Alsatian vinegars, renowned for their complexity and depth, are a staple in many kitchens. Foie gras, a delicacy made from duck or goose liver, is a testament to the region's culinary expertise. And, of course, no visit to Alsace would be complete without sampling its world-famous wines, from crisp Rieslings to aromatic Gewürztraminers. Munster cheese, a pungent and flavorful cheese made from cow's milk, is another beloved local specialty that makes for a unique and unforgettable souvenir.

Glass and Crystal: The town of Meisenthal, nestled in the heart of Alsace, is renowned for its glassblowing tradition. Skilled artisans continue to practice this ancient craft, creating exquisite glass and crystal items that range from delicate vases and bowls to intricate Christmas ornaments. These handcrafted pieces, often infused with vibrant colors and intricate designs, are treasured for their beauty and craftsmanship.

Designer Boutiques and Local Crafts: Strasbourg offers a diverse shopping scene that caters to a wide range of tastes and interests. Designer boutiques lining the city's streets showcase the latest fashion trends and unique creations by local designers. Craft stores offer a treasure trove of handmade items, from ceramics and jewelry to textiles and decorative objects. These shops provide a platform for local artisans to showcase their skills and creativity, offering visitors a chance to acquire one-of-a-kind souvenirs that embody the spirit of Alsace.

Christmas Markets: During the holiday season, Alsace's Christmas markets transform the region into a magical wonderland. These festive markets, with their twinkling lights, enchanting decorations, and cheerful atmosphere, are a feast for the senses.

Local artisans offer a wide array of handcrafted gifts, from hand-painted ornaments and wooden toys to intricately carved nativity scenes. Seasonal delicacies, such as gingerbread, mulled wine, and roasted chestnuts, fill the air with tempting aromas, creating a truly unforgettable experience.

Artisanal Soaps and Cosmetics: Alsace's artisans also excel in the creation of natural soaps and cosmetics, using traditional methods and locally sourced ingredients. These handcrafted products, often infused with the scents and essences of the region's flora, offer a luxurious and pampering experience. From lavender-infused soaps to rose-scented creams, these artisanal creations make for thoughtful and indulgent gifts.

Souvenir Shops and Beyond: For those seeking more traditional souvenirs, numerous shops throughout Alsace offer a wide selection of items that capture the essence of the region.

Postcards depicting iconic landmarks, mugs adorned with Alsatian motifs, and t-shirts featuring the region's emblem are just a few examples of the souvenirs available. Additionally, antique shops offer a glimpse into the past, with vintage wine glasses, historic cookware, and other treasures waiting to be discovered. Art galleries showcase the works of local artists, providing a platform for contemporary expressions of Alsatian culture and creativity.

Wine and Beer: No visit to Alsace would be complete without sampling the region's renowned wines and beers. Many wineries and breweries offer tastings, allowing visitors to experience the diverse flavors and aromas that define Alsatian viticulture and brewing traditions. Whether you prefer a crisp Riesling, a full-bodied Pinot Gris, or a refreshing craft beer, Alsace's liquid treasures are sure to delight your palate.

Accommodation

Hotels and Inns

Nestled in the heart of the Alsatian wine route, Hôtel Winzenberg in the quaint village of Blienschwiller is an excellent choice for discerning travelers who appreciate the finer things in life. Each well-appointed guest room features contemporary comforts, such as a private bathroom and a flat-screen TV, ensuring a pleasant and relaxing stay. Guests can enjoy complimentary WiFi throughout the property and kickstart their day with a delicious buffet breakfast served in the inviting dining room. The hotel also offers convenient bicycle rentals, enabling visitors to explore the enchanting surrounding vineyards and scenic hiking trails at their leisure.

Hotel Le Vignoble, situated in the picturesque town of Dambach-la-Ville, provides a warm and inviting "home away from home" ambiance. The hotel's comfortable rooms offer a flat-screen TV and a desk, along with complimentary WiFi, allowing guests to stay connected while enjoying their stay. The hotel boasts charming outdoor furniture and a delightful coffee shop, where guests can unwind and savor a cup of coffee or tea. Additionally, a welcoming lounge area provides a tranquil space to relax after a day of exploration. Guests traveling by car can take advantage of the complimentary parking. Conveniently located within walking distance of notable attractions like Bernstein Castle and Porte d'Ebersheim, Hotel Le Vignoble serves as an ideal base for discovering the rich cultural heritage and natural beauty of the region.

Hotel Restaurant Faller Emmebuckel, housed in a traditional Alsatian building in the village of Itterswiller, is embraced by a beautiful flowered garden with captivating vineyard views. The hotel's rooms feature a private bathroom with a shower and a flat-screen TV for guests' comfort and entertainment. The on-site restaurant tantalizes the taste buds with a menu of delectable traditional Alsatian dishes prepared with fresh, locally sourced ingredients every evening. A hearty buffet breakfast is served daily in the communal lounge, ensuring guests start their day with a satisfying meal. With free WiFi and private parking available on the premises, guests can easily embark on excursions to nearby attractions, including the majestic Château du Haut-Kœnigsbourg.

For those seeking a tranquil escape amidst the vineyards, Hôtel Restaurant Le Verger des Châteaux The Originals Relais, located near the Willy Gisselbrecht Winery in Dieffenthal, offers a serene and relaxing environment. The guest rooms are equipped with modern amenities, including flat-screen televisions, to ensure a comfortable and enjoyable stay for all visitors.

In addition to these remarkable hotels, Alsace offers a diverse array of unique accommodations to cater to different tastes and preferences. Boutique hotels like the Château d'Isenbourg in Rouffach, Hostellerie La Cheneaudière & Spa in the Bruche Valley, and Le Parc Hôtel Obernai & Spa in Obernai provide exceptional experiences, blending historical charm with contemporary luxury, world-class spa facilities, and exquisite dining options.

For budget-conscious travelers, guesthouses and B&Bs like Maison d'hôtes Les Feuilles d'Or in Eguisheim and La Cour St-Fulrad in Saint-Hippolyte offer comfortable and affordable accommodations with warm hospitality and delicious homemade breakfasts, providing a cozy home away from home for those exploring the enchanting Alsace Wine Route.

Bed and Breakfasts

Many B&Bs in Alsace are housed in meticulously restored historic properties, each one a testament to the region's rich architectural heritage. From picturesque half-timbered houses nestled in quaint villages to grand manors surrounded by sprawling vineyards, these B&Bs offer guests a chance to step back in time and experience the authentic charm of Alsace. The interiors often feature original architectural details, period furnishings, and antique accents, creating a warm and inviting atmosphere that exudes old-world elegance.

One of the hallmarks of a B&B stay is the personalized service provided by the hosts. In Alsace, B&B owners are known for their genuine warmth and hospitality, going above and beyond to ensure their guests feel welcome and comfortable. They are often eager to share their knowledge of the region, offering insider tips on local attractions, hidden gems, and off-the-beaten-path experiences. Many hosts also delight in sharing stories about the history and culture of Alsace, adding a deeper layer of understanding and appreciation to the guests' stay.

A highlight of any B&B experience is the breakfast, and in Alsace, this is no exception. Guests can expect to be treated to a delightful array of freshly baked bread, locally sourced cheeses, homemade jams, and delectable pastries, such as the region's famous kougelhopf. Some B&Bs even offer traditional Alsatian specialties like tarte flambée or choucroute garnie, providing a unique and flavorful start to the day.

The scenic locations of B&Bs in Alsace further enhance the overall experience. Whether nestled in the heart of a charming wine village, surrounded by rolling vineyards, or perched on a hillside overlooking the majestic Vosges Mountains, these accommodations offer breathtaking views and a serene ambiance. Guests can wake up to stunning vistas of the countryside, enjoy leisurely strolls through picturesque vineyards, or simply relax and soak in the tranquility of their surroundings.

For those seeking a more immersive experience, many B&Bs in Alsace offer unique opportunities to engage with the local culture. Hosts may organize wine tastings at nearby wineries, provide cooking classes where guests can learn to prepare traditional Alsatian dishes, or offer guided tours of local villages and historical landmarks. These activities allow guests to delve deeper into the region's heritage and create lasting memories.

While B&Bs in Alsace prioritize authenticity and charm, they also recognize the importance of modern comforts and amenities. Many establishments offer en-suite bathrooms, complimentary Wi-Fi access, and comfortable bedding to ensure a restful and enjoyable stay. Some B&Bs even go the extra mile by providing additional amenities such as private terraces, swimming pools, or spa facilities, further enhancing the guest experience.

Furthermore, many B&Bs in Alsace are committed to sustainability and eco-friendly practices. They may use organic linens, source their food locally, and employ renewable energy sources, such as solar power, to minimize their environmental impact. This commitment to sustainability allows guests to enjoy their stay with a clear conscience, knowing that they are supporting responsible tourism practices.

Examples of highly-rated B&Bs in Alsace include Au Coeur d'Alsace Chambres d'hotes, known for its cozy ambiance and traditional Alsatian decor, and Maison d'hôtes La Cerisaie, praised for its tranquil setting, beautifully appointed rooms, and exceptional breakfast offerings. These are just a few of the many charming B&Bs that await travelers in this enchanting region.

When planning a visit to Alsace, it is recommended to book B&B accommodations in advance, especially during peak tourist seasons. Many B&Bs are small and have limited availability, so securing reservations early ensures that you have your choice of the best options. With its unique blend of history, culture, and hospitality, a stay at a B&B in Alsace promises to be a truly unforgettable experience.

Camping and Vacation Rentals

Camping enthusiasts will find themselves spoilt for choice in Alsace, as the region boasts numerous campgrounds nestled amidst the breathtaking scenery of the Vosges Mountains or conveniently located along the famed Alsatian Wine Route. These campgrounds cater to a variety of accommodation preferences, including tents, caravans, and motorhomes. Many of them also offer additional amenities such as swimming pools, playgrounds, and on-site restaurants, ensuring a comfortable and enjoyable stay for campers of all ages.

For instance, Camping de Strasbourg, situated in close proximity to the vibrant city of Strasbourg, provides a convenient base for exploring the city and its surroundings. With a range of accommodation options, including pitches for tents and caravans as well as mobile home rentals, it caters to different needs and budgets. Alternatively, Camping Le Ried in Boofzheim offers a tranquil lakeside setting, perfect for fishing and water sports enthusiasts. Nature lovers may prefer Camping Vauban, nestled near the historic fortified town of Neuf-Brisach, where they can immerse themselves in the natural beauty of the area while having easy access to cultural attractions.

Travelers seeking a more homelike experience can opt for vacation rentals, which abound in Alsace. These rentals range from cozy cottages tucked away in the countryside to traditional half-timbered houses in charming villages, to modern apartments located in the heart of historical cities. Vacation rentals provide a sense of privacy and independence, often equipped with fully equipped kitchens and spacious living areas, allowing guests to prepare their own meals and enjoy the comforts of home while exploring the region.

Online platforms like Vrbo offer a wide selection of vacation rental properties in Alsace, catering to families, groups, and couples alike. These platforms enable travelers to easily browse and book their ideal accommodations, whether they're seeking a romantic getaway, a family vacation, or a group adventure.

Alsace also caters to thematic stays, offering a diverse range of experiences for those seeking specific interests or activities. History and culture enthusiasts can opt for renovated farmhouses or historic properties that immerse them in the region's rich heritage. Families can choose from various family-friendly campgrounds equipped with playgrounds, swimming pools, and organized activities for children. Those seeking adventure can select rentals near the hiking trails of the Vosges Mountains, providing easy access to outdoor pursuits. Additionally, cyclists can choose accommodations along the region's scenic cycling routes, allowing them to explore Alsace on two wheels.

Family-Friendly Activities

Amusement Parks

For families with young children, Cigoland - Parc des Cigognes et Attractions in Kintzheim is an excellent choice. This unique park combines entertainment with education, focusing on the conservation of the white stork, Alsace's emblematic bird. Children can enjoy a variety of rides, including canoeing and electric cars, while learning about the local fauna and flora through engaging exhibits. A highlight of the park is the aerial monorail, which provides a breathtaking view of storks nesting in their natural habitat, creating a memorable experience for visitors of all ages.

Didiland, located in Morsbronn Les Bains, is another family-friendly park that caters to a broad range of interests. Younger children can delight in ball pools and merry-go-rounds, while families can bond over water games and caravels. Thrill-seekers will find their adrenaline fix on roller coasters and log flumes, ensuring there's something for everyone in the family. Didiland also offers various entertainment options and shows, adding a festive touch to the park's atmosphere.

On hot summer days, Parc Aqua'Gonfle in Colmar provides a refreshing escape. This inflatable water park features a variety of structures and water games, making it the perfect place to cool off and have fun with friends and family.

Just across the border in Germany, near Rhinau and a short drive from Rust Europapark, Funny-World awaits families with young children. With over 50 attractions designed for children as young as one year old, including Revolverbills and Flying Sombrero, Funny-World promises a day filled with laughter and excitement for the whole family.

For a truly unique experience, Parc du Petit Prince in Ungersheim offers an aerial park inspired by Antoine de Saint-Exupéry's beloved novella. With over 30 attractions, including balloons, an aerobar, and a 3D cinema, visitors can immerse themselves in the enchanting world of the Little Prince. The park's attractions and shows are all themed around the novella's adventures, making it a must-visit for fans of the story.

While not a traditional amusement park, Parc Animalier Friedel in Illkirch-Graffenstaden offers a special experience for animal lovers and families. Visitors can wander through the park and interact with various domestic animals, such as goats, cows, and chickens. It's a wonderful opportunity to get close to nature and learn about farm life in a relaxed and enjoyable setting.

For those seeking the ultimate theme park experience, Europa-Park in Rust, Germany, is just a short distance from Alsace. As the second most popular theme park resort in Europe after Disneyland Paris, Europa-Park boasts themed areas representing different European countries, each with its own unique rides, shows, and attractions. With its diverse offerings, Europa-Park caters to all ages and interests, making it a top destination for thrill-seekers and families alike.

Zoos and Aquariums

La Montagne des Singes, also known as Monkey Mountain, is a unique sanctuary located in the charming village of Kintzheim. This extraordinary park is home to over 200 Barbary macaques, a captivating species of monkeys native to the Atlas Mountains of Algeria and Morocco. As you wander through the park's expansive grounds, you'll have the opportunity to observe these fascinating primates in a setting that closely replicates their natural habitat. Witnessing their playful interactions, intricate social dynamics, and even participating in supervised feeding sessions offers a truly immersive experience. La Montagne des Singes places a strong emphasis on conservation and education, providing valuable insights into the lives of these monkeys and the challenges they face in the wild.

Just a stone's throw away from Monkey Mountain, also in Kintzheim, lies Cigoland – Parc des Cigognes et Attractions. This unique establishment seamlessly blends entertainment with education, focusing on the stork, a bird that holds deep cultural significance in Alsace. The park offers a delightful array of attractions, including a watchtower where visitors can get up close and personal with nesting storks, a playground for children to burn off energy, and a water basin where entertaining and educational shows take place. Cigoland plays a vital role in the reintroduction of storks into the region and provides valuable information about other local wildlife, such as otters, further enriching the experience for visitors.

The Parc Zoologique & Botanique de Mulhouse, located in the city of Mulhouse, is a renowned institution that harmoniously combines the wonders of the animal kingdom with the tranquility of botanical gardens. The zoo is home to an impressive collection of over 1,200 animals representing 190 different species. As you explore the park's sprawling grounds, you'll encounter a diverse array of creatures, from majestic Siberian tigers to elusive Arctic wolves. The zoo is deeply committed to conservation efforts and actively participates in various European breeding programs, making it a vital center for the protection of endangered species.

For those particularly interested in storks, the Parc à Cigognes de Soultz / Wuenheim provides another opportunity to observe these graceful birds. Nestled between the towns of Soultz and Wuenheim, this park offers a serene environment where storks can be seen nesting, raising their young, and going about their daily routines, especially during the breeding season. The park's peaceful atmosphere allows for quiet observation and appreciation of these fascinating creatures.

Chass-guepes, while lesser-known than some of the larger zoos in the region, offers a more intimate and personalized experience with a diverse range of animals. Although smaller in scale, this zoo provides a valuable opportunity to encounter various species and learn about their unique habitats and behaviors. The close proximity to the animals allows for detailed observation and a deeper understanding of their natural instincts.

Visiting these zoos and animal parks in Alsace not only provides a delightful and educational experience but also contributes to the conservation and well-being of the animals. Each location offers its own unique set of attractions, ranging from interactive feeding sessions to informative educational programs, ensuring that visitors of all ages can learn about and appreciate the wonders of the natural world.

Interactive Museums

The Écomusée d'Alsace, nestled in the village of Ungersheim, stands as a testament to the region's commitment to preserving its cultural heritage. As France's largest open-air museum, it transports visitors back in time to an early 20th-century Alsatian village. The museum boasts an impressive collection of buildings, meticulously reconstructed and furnished to reflect the everyday life of the past. Visitors can wander through the village, exploring authentic homes, workshops, and communal spaces, gaining a deeper understanding of traditional Alsatian life.

The Écomusée d'Alsace also showcases a diverse array of everyday artifacts, tools, and machinery, offering insights into the skills and craftsmanship of bygone eras. Throughout the museum, knowledgeable guides and artisans demonstrate traditional crafts and trades, allowing visitors to witness the techniques and artistry that have been passed down through generations. With its sprawling grounds encompassing over 97 hectares of natural landscapes, the Écomusée d'Alsace offers ample opportunities for exploration and discovery. Visitors can encounter a variety of farm animals, participate in workshops and demonstrations, and even enjoy seasonal events and festivals that celebrate Alsatian traditions.

The Mulhouse Tourist Office serves as a valuable resource for those interested in exploring the Écomusée d'Alsace and other cultural attractions in the region. It provides comprehensive information about the museum's exhibits, events, and educational programs, ensuring that visitors can make the most of their experience. The tourist office emphasizes the interactive nature of the Écomusée, highlighting the opportunity to witness history come to life through the restored buildings, artifacts, and demonstrations. Visitors are encouraged to engage with the artisans and learn about their trades, from pottery and weaving to blacksmithing and carpentry. The museum's immersive environment allows visitors to truly step back in time and gain a deeper appreciation for the rich heritage of Alsace.

In addition to the Écomusée d'Alsace, the region boasts a plethora of other interactive museums that cater to various interests. Fun and family-oriented activities abound, offering playful ways to learn and explore. Children and adults alike can participate in exciting science experiments, embark on archaeological digs, or even try their hand at traditional crafts. These hands-on experiences foster a deeper understanding and appreciation for the region's history and culture, making learning an engaging and enjoyable adventure.

Alsace is home to over 150 museums, each with its unique focus and collection. Tripadvisor's list of the 10 Best Museums in Alsace provides a valuable resource for those seeking diverse perspectives on the region's culture. These museums cover a wide range of topics, from architecture, religion, and folklore to art, science, and technology. Visitors can delve into the intricacies of Alsatian traditions, explore the region's artistic heritage, and discover the scientific and technological advancements that have shaped its history.

Day Trips and Excursions

Nearby Destinations

Across the Rhine River in Germany, the Black Forest entices with its dense, evergreen forests and picturesque villages. This region is renowned for its cuckoo clocks, traditional wooden houses, and the legendary Black Forest cake. Hiking and mountain biking trails crisscross the forest, offering endless opportunities for outdoor adventure.

A short trip to Switzerland reveals the vibrant city of Basel, a cultural hub known for its world-class museums, including the renowned Kunstmuseum Basel, and its annual Art Basel fair, a major event in the international art world. The city's Old Town, with its historic architecture and charming squares, is a delight to explore.

Freiburg, another German city close to Alsace, exudes a unique charm with its medieval minster and commitment to sustainable living. It serves as a gateway to the Black Forest and offers a delightful blend of history, culture, and environmental consciousness.

To the west of Alsace, the cities of Nancy and Metz boast rich histories and impressive architectural heritage. Nancy's Place Stanislas, a UNESCO World Heritage site, is a masterpiece of 18th-century architecture, while Metz's Saint-Stephen Cathedral is renowned for its stunning stained-glass windows, including works by Marc Chagall.

Suggested Itineraries

A journey through Alsace promises to be a captivating experience, blending the richness of cultural heritage, the allure of natural landscapes, and the indulgence of gastronomical delights. This suggested itinerary is designed to guide you through the best that Alsace has to offer, ensuring a memorable exploration of this picturesque region in France.

Day 1: Embark on your Alsatian adventure in Strasbourg, the vibrant capital city. The morning beckons you to marvel at the architectural grandeur of the Strasbourg Cathedral, a Gothic masterpiece that has stood the test of time. Ascend the cathedral's tower for a breathtaking panoramic vista of the cityscape.

Venture into the heart of Strasbourg's history as you explore the Grande Île, a UNESCO World Heritage site that exudes charm and character. Lose yourself in the enchanting labyrinthine streets of La Petite France, a quarter that seems to have sprung from the pages of a fairy tale.

For lunch, treat your taste buds to the authentic flavors of Alsace by indulging in traditional dishes such as choucroute garnie at a local restaurant nestled in a historic wine cellar. The afternoon invites you to embark on a delightful boat tour along the serene River Ill, offering a unique perspective of Strasbourg's architectural treasures.

Day 2: The second day calls for a scenic journey along the renowned Alsace Wine Route. Begin your exploration in Obernai, a town celebrated for its impeccably preserved medieval architecture. Venture into the heart of the region's viticulture as you visit local wineries, where you can sample the celebrated Riesling and Gewürztraminer wines that have made Alsace famous.

Continue your wine-infused journey to Barr and Mittelbergheim, two charming villages enveloped by sprawling vineyards. Immerse yourself in the tranquility of the countryside as you stroll through the vineyards and soak in the picturesque scenery.

Conclude your day in Dambach-la-Ville, another captivating village that boasts a rich winemaking tradition. Partake in a wine tasting session to further your appreciation of Alsatian wines and gain insights into the intricate process of viticulture.

Day 3: The third day is dedicated to discovering the majestic castles and quaint villages that dot the Alsatian landscape. Begin with a visit to the Château du Haut-Koenigsbourg, a meticulously restored medieval castle that commands breathtaking views of the Vosges Mountains and the Rhine Valley.

Journey onward to Riquewihr, a village that appears to have been frozen in time. Its cobblestone streets, half-timbered houses, and colorful facades transport you to a bygone era, offering a glimpse into the region's rich history.

Conclude your day in Kaysersberg, a village that has captured the hearts of many and was even voted "France's Favorite Village" in 2017. Explore its historic center, where you'll encounter architectural gems and the remnants of the Kaysersberg Castle.

Day 4: The final day of your Alsatian escapade brings you to Colmar, a town often referred to as "Little Venice" due to its charming network of canals. Immerse yourself in the art world with a visit to the Unterlinden Museum, where you can admire the renowned Isenheim Altarpiece.

Don't miss the Bartholdi Museum, a tribute to the sculptor who created the iconic Statue of Liberty. As evening descends, take a leisurely stroll through the old town, where you can savor a delectable dinner at one of the traditional "winstubs" and sample local specialties like the mouthwatering Tarte Flambée.

This itinerary merely scratches the surface of what Alsace has to offer. The region is a treasure trove of experiences, from its quaint villages nestled amidst lush vineyards to its rich culinary traditions.

Travel Tips

Packing Guide

Clothing

Alsace experiences a semi-temperate climate, characterized by mild summers and fairly cold winters. In the warmer months, pack lightweight, breathable clothing such as t-shirts, shorts, skirts, and dresses. Include a light jacket or sweater for cooler evenings or unexpected rain showers. If your itinerary involves outdoor activities like hiking or cycling, consider packing moisture-wicking fabrics and quick-drying materials.

As the weather turns colder, be sure to pack warm layers, including sweaters, long-sleeved shirts, and pants. A heavy coat, gloves, a scarf, and a hat are essential for winter travel, as temperatures can drop significantly. If you plan to visit during the shoulder seasons of spring or autumn, pack a mix of warm and cool-weather clothing to accommodate the unpredictable temperatures.

Footwear

Comfortable footwear is essential for exploring Alsace's charming villages, cobblestone streets, and scenic vineyards.

Pack a sturdy pair of walking shoes or hiking boots, especially if you plan to venture into the Vosges Mountains or enjoy outdoor activities. For evenings out or visits to restaurants and cultural events, consider packing a pair of dress shoes or sandals to complete your outfit.

Essentials

Don't forget the essentials for any international trip. Ensure you have your passport, identification documents, travel insurance papers, and any necessary visas. While credit cards are widely accepted in Alsace, it's wise to carry some cash in euros for smaller establishments or rural areas where card payments may not be available.

Health and safety should also be a priority. Pack a basic first aid kit containing bandages, pain relievers, and any necessary medications. If you have any specific medical conditions, be sure to bring enough medication for the duration of your trip. Hand sanitizer and masks may still be required in some settings, so pack them accordingly.

Gadgets

Capture the beauty of Alsace with a good camera or ensure your smartphone has ample storage space for your photos. Don't forget to bring a power adapter compatible with France's Type E power sockets to keep your electronic devices charged. A portable charger is also a handy item to have, allowing you to charge your phone or camera on the go, especially if you plan to be out exploring for extended periods.

Miscellaneous

A comfortable daypack is essential for carrying your essentials during daily excursions. Pack a reusable water bottle to stay hydrated while reducing plastic waste. An umbrella or raincoat will come in handy in case of unexpected rain showers, which are common in Alsace, particularly during the spring and autumn months.

If you're a wine enthusiast, consider packing a protective wine carrier to safely transport any bottles you may purchase along the Alsace Wine Route. A corkscrew will also be useful if you wish to enjoy a bottle in your hotel room or during a picnic.

Cultural Considerations

While many people in Alsace speak English, it's always appreciated when visitors make an effort to speak some French. Pack a French phrasebook or download a language app to help you communicate with locals and navigate the region. A detailed guidebook about Alsace will provide valuable insights into its history, culture, and attractions, enhancing your overall experience.

Seasonal Items

In the summer, protect yourself from the sun with sunscreen, sunglasses, and a hat. If you're visiting in winter, thermal layers, a scarf, and insulated boots are essential to stay warm and comfortable.

Etiquette and Customs

Greetings and Social Etiquette

In Alsace, greetings are a fundamental aspect of social interaction. When meeting someone for the first time, a firm handshake is the norm, accompanied by direct eye contact and a genuine smile. Among friends and family, the customary greeting is "la bise," a series of light kisses on both cheeks, starting with the right. It's essential to address people using their proper titles, such as "Monsieur" or "Madame," unless invited to use first names, as this demonstrates respect for their position and social standing.

Language

French is the official language of Alsace, and while many locals speak English, especially in tourist areas, making an effort to speak a few phrases in French will be greatly appreciated. The Alsatian dialect, a Germanic language spoken by many residents, adds another layer to the region's linguistic landscape. Even a few words in Alsatian can go a long way in building rapport and establishing a connection with the local people.

Dining Etiquette

Alsatian dining experiences are a delightful fusion of French sophistication and German heartiness. If you're invited to a meal at someone's home, it's customary to bring a small gift, such as a bottle of wine or a bouquet of flowers, as a gesture of appreciation. Meals in Alsace are often leisurely affairs, and it's considered polite to wait for the host to propose a toast before taking your first sip. During the meal, keep your hands visible on the table, as placing them on your lap is generally frowned upon.

Engage in conversation and show interest in the local cuisine, as this will be well-received by your hosts.

Dress Code

Alsatians take pride in their appearance and tend to dress smartly, even in casual settings. While there's no need to be overly formal, it's best to avoid wearing overly revealing or beachwear in public places. If you're visiting a religious site, such as a church or cathedral, dressing modestly is essential out of respect for the local customs and traditions.

Festivals and Celebrations

Alsace is renowned for its vibrant festivals and celebrations that showcase the region's unique cultural identity. From the colorful "corsos fleuris," where flower-decked floats parade through the streets, to the lively "La fête de l'Ami Fritz," a celebration filled with music, dance, and traditional food, these events offer a glimpse into the heart and soul of Alsace. Participating in these festivities is a fantastic way to immerse yourself in the local culture and create lasting memories.

Wine and Beer

Alsace is a world-renowned wine region, and its winemaking traditions are deeply intertwined with its culture and history. When visiting wineries or participating in wine tastings, it's polite to show appreciation for the winemaker's expertise and express interest in the winemaking process. Similarly, Alsace is also home to a thriving beer culture, with numerous local breweries producing a wide array of unique and flavorful brews. Sampling these local specialties is a must for any beer enthusiast visiting the region.

Art and Architecture

Alsace boasts a remarkable architectural heritage, with influences from both French and German styles. Half-timbered houses, ornate churches, and imposing castles dot the landscape, each telling a story of the region's rich past. Taking the time to appreciate the intricate details and historical significance of these structures is a meaningful way to connect with the local culture.

Shopping and Business

When shopping in local markets or shops, polite bargaining is acceptable, but avoid aggressive haggling. In business settings, punctuality is highly valued, and it's customary to dress professionally. Building relationships and establishing trust are key components of successful business interactions in Alsace.

Environmental Consciousness

Alsace has a strong tradition of environmental consciousness, and locals take pride in preserving their natural surroundings. Recycling is widely practiced, and energy conservation is a priority. As a visitor, respecting these practices and minimizing your environmental impact is a way to show your appreciation for the region's commitment to sustainability.

Emergency Contacts

The primary emergency number in France, and indeed throughout Europe, is 112. This pan-European emergency number acts as a central hub, connecting you to the relevant emergency service, whether it's medical, fire, or police. The 112 number can be dialed free of charge from any phone, including mobile phones, landlines, and payphones, making it easily accessible in any emergency situation. Additionally, while 911 is the primary emergency number in the United States, dialing it in France will typically redirect you to the 112 service.

For more specific emergencies, France has dedicated numbers for different services. Dialing 15 will connect you to SAMU, the emergency medical service. This number should be used in cases of urgent medical needs, such as accidents, sudden illnesses, or life-threatening conditions. The police can be reached by dialing 17, and this number is appropriate for reporting crimes, disturbances, or any situation that requires immediate law enforcement intervention. In the event of a fire, accident, or rescue situation, dialing 18 will connect you to the Sapeurs Pompiers, the fire and rescue service.

France also provides specialized emergency services to cater to specific needs. For individuals with hearing impairments, the 114 number offers hearing-assisted emergency services, accessible via SMS and fax. If you are facing a social emergency or require immediate shelter, the 115 number can provide assistance. Child protection services can be reached by dialing 119 if you suspect a child is in danger or being abused. In cases of missing children, the 116 000 number is dedicated to reporting and providing assistance. For medical help outside of regular doctor's office hours, the 116 117 service is available.

Emergencies at sea or on lakes can be reported by dialing 196 if calling from land, or 112 or VHF Channel 16 if calling from a boat. For air rescue services, 191 is the designated number. To find a pharmacy that is open outside of normal hours, you can call 32 37, especially useful at night, on Sundays, or during public holidays. In the unfortunate event of a terror attack or kidnapping, the dedicated hotline 197 is available for immediate assistance.

It's important to note that while emergency operators in France may speak English, there's no guarantee of English-language service. Therefore, it's helpful to familiarize yourself with some basic French phrases related to emergencies. When calling for help, remember to clearly state the location of the emergency, your name, and contact information. Provide accurate and detailed information about the situation, including the number of people involved and any potential hazards, such as weapons or dangerous substances.

Remember that all emergency numbers in France can be dialed from payphones without the need for a phone card or money. Even if your mobile phone is locked, you can still access emergency services. In any emergency, staying calm, providing clear information, and following the instructions of the emergency operators can be crucial in ensuring a swift and effective response.

Printed in Great Britain
by Amazon